PRAISE
A LA CARTE

*Nourishment for body and soul
from my kitchen to yours*

KAY D. RIZZO

PACIFIC PRESS PUBLISHING ASSOCIATION
Nampa, Idaho
Oshawa, Ontario, Canada

Edited by Jerry D. Thomas
Designed by Michelle C. Petz

© 1996 by
Pacific Press Publishing Association
Printed in the United States of America
All Rights Reserved

Rizzo, Kay D.
    Praise a la carte: nourishment for body and soul from my kitchen to yours / Kay D. Rizzo.
        p.   cm.
    Includes index.
    ISBN 0-8163-1353-9
    1. Cookery. 2. Christian Life. I. Title.
    TX652.R58 1997
    641.5—dc20   96-19404
                                                                        CIP

96 97 98 99 00 • 5 4 3 2 1

Dedication

To my precious daughter,
Rhonda Kay Ringering,
a far better cook than her mother!

Table of Contents

Introduction

"Praise the Lord, O my soul; all my inmost being, praise his holy name.
Praise the Lord, O my soul, and forget not all his benefits"
(Psalm 103:1, #2, NIV).

Just what the world needs—another cookbook!

Bookstore shelves groan under the weight of new and not-so-new cookbooks. Each one has its own unique twist, everything from "Cooking with Pasta" to "Cooking With Booze" to "Cooking With Friends."

How is *Praise a la Carte* different? The title says it all. Praise is more than humming a happy little tune as you work. It goes beyond a perky smile. It's more than a change of attitude: it's a change of heart.

"Forget not his benefits," the Bible verse says. That's the gratitude part—remembering our past and God's leading in it. As one inspired writer put it, "We have nothing to fear for the future, lest we forget how God has led us in the past." Now that's a reason for giving thanks!

Put our praise and our thanksgiving together with the food we eat, and "voila" as the French say, we have a luscious recipe for joy that is heart smart, both physically and spiritually—a winning combination that is guaranteed to please the most discriminating of palates! Read for yourself God's recipe for joyful eating.

"Go and enjoy choice food . . .
for the joy of the Lord is your strength"
(Nehemiah 8:10, NIV).

"Go, eat your food with gladness, and drink your wine with a joyful heart,
for it is now that God favors what you do"
(Ecclesiastes 9:7, NIV).

"Whether you eat or drink or whatever you do,
do it all for the glory of God"
(1 Corinthians 10:31, NIV).

Come on over to my house for a visit or two. Make yourself at home. Share my kitchen. Peek into the cupboards of my mind. Grab a dipper and fill your bowl with a hearty stew of praise. Sprinkle on a generous portion of thanskgiving. And give God the glory!

Notes

Rizzo Family Salad

*"We will tell the next generation the praiseworthy deeds of the Lord,
his power, and the wonders he has done"*
(Psalm 78:4, NIV).

"Italian tossed salad dressing—a Rizzo specialty—is one of those inherited no-recipe recipes. Just the right amount of onion powder, salt, olive oil, garlic powder, and fresh lemons—nothing fancy, just mouth-watering good. For variety, add to the crisp green lettuce a tomato or two, cucumbers, croutons, cheese chunks, or sunflower seeds, according to the cook's own taste" (*Gospel in the Grocery Store*).

Since I wrote the above excerpt in 1988, the fame of Rizzo salads has spread. Not only family members call and say, "Get out the salad fixings; we're coming for a visit," but church members and long-treasured friends, as well. I love it!

My husband has become somewhat of a cult hero at our local church potlucks. First, because it is so rare to have a man invade the women's domain, and second, because he has taught them how to make the dressing for their families. Teenage boys in the congregation hoping to "snatch" a seasoned leaf or two, hover around him in the church kitchen as he creates his masterpiece.

As a teenager growing up in Brooklyn, New York, Richard learned to make the dressing from his mother, a second-generation American. When we married, he shared the recipe with me, a woman of English descent. And after much trial and error, I can now produce a suitably Italian "Rizzo" salad. As our two girls grew into helping in the kitchen, Richard passed the skill on to them. Married to two great guys, Rhonda and Kelli continue the Rizzo salad tradition in their own kitchens.

Over the years, I've discovered an interesting anomaly. All of us use the same ingredients. We each mix and blend the ingredients in approximately the same order and amounts. Yet our salads taste distinctly different from one another. Kelli's salad doesn't taste like mine, my salad has a different flavor than Rhonda's, and Grandma's isn't anything like Richard's. Each is different and special.

And to the girls, no one's salad is quite like Dad's. When they come to visit, it's his salad they request.

"Unto the third and fourth generation . . ." A simple thing like the recipe for a family salad can span many generations. That's not so unusual. Many families have treasured recipes, passed from mother to daughter to daughter, and so forth.

As any Christian parent will tell you, more than just salad or cake or pudding recipes span the generations. Attitudes toward God and toward others, habits that enrich and habits that destroy; tendencies, talents, and temperaments are passed on as well.

As offspring of the heavenly King, Richard and I wanted to pass on another important recipe to our daughters: a recipe for Christian living—a life seasoned with joy and victory. We inherited these treasured secrets from our parents and pray that we have successfully transferred them to our offspring.

Today, I can see the variations in that same "living" recipe as it is produced in the lives of the next generation. Like the subtle variations in the Rizzo family salad—more onion, less lemon, a second squirt of olive oil—there are differences in how each of them live. But, praise God, the basic ingredients of faith, peace, and love continue from generation to generation as strong and as flavorful as ever.

1 medium bunch
romaine lettuce

1 to 1½ tsp. salt

1 scant tsp. garlic
(powdered or minced)

2 tsp. onion (powdered)

Optional ingredients:

1 tsp. sweet basil
1 tsp. oregano
tomatoes
cheese chunks
cucumbers
black olives
etc.

1 to 3 lemons
(according to taste)

1 to 2 Tbsp. olive oil

Rizzo Family Salad

[SALAD FOR 2]

Wash the lettuce and tear the leaves into bite-sized pieces. Toss in a salad bowl, with salt, garlic, onion, and the optional ingredients of your choice. Then cut the lemons in half and squeeze lemon juice into the salad. After you toss it again, add oil and keep tossing! (If you are including croutons, add them at this time.) Serve with generous amounts of laughter and love.

Experiment with the quantities of the ingredients to satisfy your own taste. Make it your family salad!

Swamp Salad

An old swamp fisherman's adage says, "The swamp is like a mother; she never fails her children." Before I visited my nephew and his wife in east Texas, my knowledge of swamps came from books and films. They were dark, uninhabitable places alive with disease, danger, and death. I learned, as we putted along through the trees, that swampland is the most life-filled place on the planet. Abundant life! From the graceful damselfly preening on a water lily to a submerged alligator lurking in the shadows, the variety was endless.

Birds rattled, creaked, and groaned instead of chirping. They sounded more like rusty hinges than cooing doves. Egrets lifted their regal heads above prairie grasses, inspecting us as we passed. Cypress knees rose from the swamp's waters, mysterious forms reaching as high as five feet. Botanists have never been able to discover their function. Spanish moss hung in clusters from the branches, and also—in the water and in full color—from upside-down trees.

Incredible. Out of decay and death, life springs. Makes you think of Jesus, doesn't it? To the pure Son of God, my life must have looked like a decaying, germ-infested swamp. Then one day, He came to me and said, "I have come that you might have life; and that you might have it, more abundantly." Praise God! He can create life where there was only death, and victory where decay once ruled supreme. And He does it in abundance! Full and running over with heavenly abundance!

As if forgiveness and cleansing weren't enough, I can depend on the Father to keep His word. Just as the swamp never fails her children, so my Daddy God never will fail me (*see Hebrews 13:5*).

stale bread

vegetable possibilities:

yellow, red, and purple
peppers
red onions
cucumbers
zucchini
tomatoes (diced)

parsley and basil

cheese

. . . .

Simple dressing:

½ tsp. garlic powder

1 tsp. onion powder

1 tsp. salt

6 Tbsp. olive oil

2 Tbsp. lemon

Swamp Salad

[I KNOW IT SOUNDS STRANGE—BUT TRY IT!]

Place two slices of stale bread into bowl of warm water—just enough to moisten both sides.

Break up the bread. Squeeze the water out of the bread and crumble the bread into a salad bowl.

Add 1 cup of each fresh, chopped vegetable of your choice. Personally, I like yellow, red, and purple peppers, red onions, cucumbers, zucchini, and tomatoes (diced).

Add fresh, chopped parsley and basil to taste. Now toss!

Shake the dressing up and allow the ingredients to marinate in the jar for 30 to 60 minutes. Pour this over the vegetables and bread mixture. Toss, sprinkle with grated cheese, and serve. You'll be glad you did!

Ants on a Log

*"He said to them, 'Let the little children come to me, and do not hinder them,
for the kingdom of God belongs to such as these'"
(Mark 10:14, NIV).*

For four magical years, the Rizzo family lived in a converted hunting lodge on the edge of a mountain. A master bedroom with bath and a sunken parlor had been added onto the original two-bedroom tin-roofed cabin.

The cabin's open-beamed kitchen and dining area awed everyone who visited. The warm honey-brown pine wall paneling came from the mountain behind us. A huge stone fireplace, which filled a major portion of one wall, could easily accommodate four-foot logs. Above an antique dining table, a graceful chandelier hung suspended from one of the exposed beams.

On cool autumn days and frosty winter mornings, steam coated the small-paned cottage windows that dotted the wall opposite the fireplace. In the summer, the top half of a red dutch door swung open, welcoming my daughters' shouts and laughter as they played on the cool green lawn.

The kitchen, separated from the dining area by an island counter and sink, was an ideal spot for little hands to discover the joy of "cooking." Whether it be "bread-making day" or creating Christmas cookies or Valentine's Day gelatin shapes, there was room for adults and kids to work in harmony.

17

Too often kitchens are designed to prevent children from participating in the preparation process, from enjoying the company of Mom or Dad. Today, as I remember our good times around that island counter, I thank God for the woman who designed that special kitchen.

While the following recipe is new to me, it's one I wish I'd had when Rhonda and Kelli were young and we lived in our "little house in the big woods." Even the littlest hands can create this one.

2 stalks celery

2 Tbsp. light cream cheese

1 Tbsp. raisins or
mixed dried fruit

Ants on a Log

Cut the celery stalks into four-inch segments. Then spread cream cheese down the center of each stalk. Top the cream cheese with raisins or dried fruit pieces, and there they are—ants on a log!

Asian Salad

"Carry each other's burdens,
and in this way you will fulfill the law of Christ"
(Galatians 6:2, NIV).

One of the perks of my profession is being invited to speak at women's retreats around the country. Why people believe that if you can write you can speak, I do not know. But that's how it is and how I started my career in public speaking—through my book *Gospel in the Grocery Store*. When I first heard about women's ministries, I closed my eyes and shuddered. *"E-e-eugh!"* I thought. *"Why would I want to spend an entire weekend in the company of only women? Aren't there enough divisions in our church already without creating another?"*

My eyes were opened when I was invited to speak at my first retreat, the Idaho Women's Retreat. I attended, thinking I would hate every minute of my time there. The opposite happened. Old and young—financially, ethnically, and educationally diverse—the women of Idaho loved me right into their hearts.

I met young mothers, struggling alone to raise their children as God intended. I spoke with older women, caught between a rigid husband and their adult children, trying to hold their families together. I listened to women of differing ages reveal horrendous stories of abuse: physical, emotional, sexual, and spiritual. I saw spiritually strong women carrying incredible burdens; searching women asking questions they'd never ask in the presence of a man; growing women sharing the secrets to their victorious walk with their Saviour; hungry women starving for the friendship of caring women.

Yes, I came home changed. As a result, I could hardly wait to attend my next women's retreat. Since then, I've enjoyed dozens of similar retreats. And every time, I return home carrying a bouquet of new friends, a heart overflowing with a renewed love for my Saviour, and fresh understanding of my sisters-in-Christ.

I am so thankful that some Christian woman somewhere said, "Wouldn't it be nice if women had a way to get together and support one another in Christ?" Praise God! My only question is, "Why did it take so long?"

Now, I eagerly anticipate every opportunity to join my sisters in a weekend of friendship and praise. While I always come home with new friends and new ideas, I often return to California with a new recipe. The following recipe came from the 1994 Florida Conference Women's Retreat at Camp Kolaqua. Pat Shanko, my friend and my hostess for the weekend, shared it with me.

Asian Salad

2 packages of
Ramen noodle mix,
oriental style

½ cup margarine

1 lb. cabbage/carrot slaw

4 green onions, diced

¾ cup slivered almonds

½ cup sesame or sun-
flower seeds

. . . .

Dressing:

5 tsp. vinegar

½ cup vegetable oil

3 Tbsp. sugar

2 tsp. soy sauce

1 packet seasoning
from noodles

Set aside the flavor packets from the noodle packages; then melt the margarine in a hot skillet. Break the dry noodles into the skillet and brown them until they appear a light tan color—stirring often. Then allow the noodles to cool.

Mix the dressing ingredients well just before serving. Stir the dressing and pour it over the cabbage and onions. Then add the almonds and seeds. Finally, toss it all again and serve it on individual lettuce leaves.

Fresh Spinach Toss-up

"Who is it that overcomes the world?
Only he who believes that Jesus is the Son of God"
(1 John 5:5, NIV).

My hubby loves most fruits and vegetables. Over the years, he's been easy to please when it comes to food. He credits the four years he ate in college cafeterias for his accepting attitude. If he'd come to my table directly from his mother's, I fear it would not have been so. However, the very sight of cooked spinach will cause his nose to wrinkle. Fresh? Fine, but cooked, "Don't even try."

When we added baby food to our first child's diet, I experimented with different fruits and vegetables. She gobbled them down with enthusiasm, until she came to spinach. We still have the photographs of Rhonda's first taste of pulverized spinach. The scrunched-up button nose told us, "Like father, like daughter."

Her tiny pink tongue pushed the concoction from her mouth. Scooping it into her spoon, I stuffed it back in. Again, she spewed it out. Cleaning it from her face, I tried a fresh spoonful. She repeated the performance. No way was that five-month-old child going to willingly swallow the ghastly green mixture. I decided to wait a few months, then try again. The only change was the weather outside our kitchen window. Rhonda still maintained her dislike for spinach.

Over the years, while Richard's dislike of cooked spinach has remained the same, Rhonda's has changed. She now enjoys spinach as much as the rest of us.

Sometimes it's easy to believe that the tastes and tendencies we inherit from our parents are permanent, impossible to change. We shrug our shoulders and say, "What can I do about it? My dad was the same."

But Jesus said, "I have overcome the world." Praise God! He can overcome our love for the bad and our dislike of the good, if we let Him. Liking or disliking cooked spinach is unimportant in the general pattern of our lives. It is the attitude of blaming our parents and grandparents for our problems, which keeps us from giving over our habits and inherited tendencies to God.

Maybe the problem is a complaining spirit, alcoholism, gossip, self-dependency, criticism. So what if Grandpa and Grandma suffered from the same bad trait? By giving it to the Father and by seeking His will for your life, even the knottiest of problems can be unraveled.

As you prepare Fresh Spinach Toss-up for those you love, pray as you toss the spinach leaves. Thank God for the gifts your family passed on to you—good and bad. Then, ask the One who overcame the world to reveal to you whatever "spinach" attitudes you may have that need adjusting.

Fresh Spinach Toss-up

1 Tbsp. margarine

12 cups fresh spinach, torn

1 Tbsp. olive oil

1 clove garlic—minced

½ tsp. salt

3 cups raisins

½ cup nuts, chopped

1 Tbsp. shredded Parmesan cheese

In a small microwavable bowl, melt the margarine on 100 percent power (high) for 30 to 40 seconds; then set it aside.

In a 3-quart microwavable casserole dish, combine the oil, garlic, salt, raisins, and nuts. Cover and microwave on high for 1 minute.

Add the spinach and the melted margarine. Toss the spinach until it is coated (don't forget to pray!).

Cover the dish and microwave it until the spinach is wilted (heated throughout)—2 to 3 minutes. Sprinkle the spinach with cheese (if you wish) before serving.

Notes

"Do Yourself a Favor" Lentil Soup

*"Be content with what you have, because God has said,
'Never will I leave you; never will I forsake you'"
(Hebrews 13:5, NIV).*

At the first hint of autumn, I haul my hot pot from the back of the cupboard, wash it to remove the dust collected from a summertime of living in the San Joaquin Valley, and fill it with hot water. I am heading back to my northern roots—it's homemade soup day. Not only does the soup bring back treasured memories of frosted windowpanes and icicles dangling from the eaves, but also the memories of babies building block castles and little girls playing dolls on the floor behind me.

As delicious aromas waft through the house, I remember when homemade lentil soup had more to do with finances than nostalgia. The necessity of living on a sparse budget helped me go creative with lentils. In addition to lentil soup, I made roasts, patties, casseroles, and sandwiches. I used to joke that I could write a cookbook entitled *150 Ways With Lentils*.

As our financial picture improved, we found ourselves eating fewer lentil dishes and more prepared foods. Yet, the moment a golden leaf flutters past my kitchen window—the instant the temperature drops below sixty degrees—my thoughts return to lentils and my "Do Yourself a Favor" Lentil Soup.

The lentil soup not only tastes good, warming the "cockles of my heart," but is so very good for us. As my husband, Richard, finishes his third bowl, he always says, "Listen! Listen to my heart. It's saying 'Thank you.'"

Of our five senses, scientists tell us that our senses of smell and taste evoke the strongest memories. What a tragedy it is to lose one's memories of the events of the past, of the good times with family and friends. What a greater tragedy it is to forget what God has done for us. If we forget how God has led us in the past, we can have no joy, no praise, and no faith in tomorrow.

He promised, "Never will I leave you; never will I forsake you" (Hebrews 13:5). Do yourself a favor today. Praise Him for His everlasting love. And enjoy a bowl of lentil soup.

1 lb. lentils

1 large onion, minced

1 cup celery, minced

3 Tbsp. olive oil

16 oz. can tomatoes

2 cloves garlic, minced

8 oz. package
chopped spinach

½ cup uncooked rice
(optional)

salt to taste

grated Parmesan cheese
(optional)

"Do Yourself a Favor" Lentil Soup

[**MAKES 4-6 SERVINGS**]

On the Stove

Wash the lentils; then cover them with boiling water and cook for one hour over medium heat. Then sauté the onion and celery in oil. Add them to the lentils, along with the tomatoes, garlic, and spinach.

Cook them all together for one more hour, until the lentils are soft. Then add the rice and cook it all for an additional 20 to 30 minutes. Garnish the results with Parmesan cheese, if you wish.

In the Hot Pot

Fill your hot pot 3/4 full of water. Add your washed lentils, onions, celery, tomatoes, garlic, and spinach and cook on high for no less than two hours, no more than four hours.

For a thicker soup, add the rice and cook for an additional 30 minutes to an hour. Garnish with grated cheese, if you wish.

For variety, I substitute cubed potatoes for the rice or throw in a handful of green beans and sliced carrots.

Pasta e Fagioli

"The Spirit himself testifies with our spirit that we are God's children.
Now if we are children, then we are . . . heirs of God and co-heirs with Christ"
(Romans 8:16, 17, NIV).

Growing up in Brooklyn, New York, one of Richard's favorite memories of his father was taking the Culder Line train to Coney Island every Tuesday evening during the summer. The excursion would include one ride on the merry-go-round and a free seat to watch the fireworks over the bay. The father and son would stroll along the boardwalk talking about nothing, and yet, everything. Kelli and Richard established a similar tradition on the Fourth of July during her teenage years. Since she married and established her own home, Richard grows nostalgic every Fourth of July.

Another memory Richard talks about again and again is centered around eating pasta e fagioli. When Mama Rizzo made the delicious Italian pasta and bean soup, Richard and his father would have hot chili pepper contests. They would slice the chilies into the mild-flavored soup to determine who could eat more chunks of chili pepper. As tears streamed down their faces, neither would willingly concede. In the background, Mama would be wringing her hands and predicting they'd burn out their stomach linings. "And then you'll be happy," she added.

Papa Rizzo probably never knew how special these memories would become to his youngest son. Like most parents, Papa Rizzo wanted to give his son the best. If money had been available, he would have been overjoyed to take Richard and his brother and sister to Italy where he grew up or to Rome or to Florence where Mama Rizzo's ancestors resided. But alas, there was no money for such an excursion. Instead, Papa Rizzo gave Richard his best—he gave himself.

Whenever I hear about tours of the Holy Land, I fantasize about making such a journey. What must it be like to walk the same dusty trails that Jesus walked or wade into the waters of the River Jordan where He was baptized? To walk the Via Dolorosa and climb the hill of Calvary? To visit a carpenter's shop in Nazareth or a stable in Bethlehem?

I sigh when I realize that there is no money available for such a journey. But you know what? It doesn't really matter. For my Saviour understands what Papa Rizzo understood.

Everyday my loving Lord gives me His best—Himself. We do simple everyday things together, watch sunsets, wash dishes, pull weeds in the garden, eat pasta e fagioli—together. We talk about everything imaginable. And His Words thrill me again and again.

Spending time together—that's what parenting is all about, whether it's human parenting or God-parenting. Aren't you glad we love a Daddy like that?"

1 large onion, chopped

3 cloves garlic, minced

½ cup celery, diced

¼ cup olive oil

16 oz. can stewed tomatoes

2 Tbsp. tomato paste,
diluted with ½ cup water

¼ tsp. dried oregano

¼ dried sweet basil

salt to taste

8 cups water

1 cup of elbow macaroni

8 oz. can
garbanzo beans

chili peppers (optional)

Pasta e Fagioli

[**MAKES 6-8 SERVINGS**]

Heat the olive oil in a large skillet. Add the onion, garlic, and celery. Sauté everything until the celery is soft (5 to 7 minutes). Next, add the tomatoes, tomato paste, oregano, basil, and salt and let it simmer for 15 minutes. Then remove the pan from heat and set it aside.

Put the water into a large saucepan and bring it to a boil. Add the macaroni and cook until it is tender (12 to 15 minutes).

Drain the garbanzo beans and add them to the macaroni, along with the sauce mixture. Add salt to suit your taste. Finally, bring it all to a boil and then let it simmer until time to serve.

Serve with chili peppers (optional!)

Marinara Sauce

*"Blessed are those who hunger and thirst for righteousness,
for they will be filled"
(Matthew 5:6, NIV).*

Nothing is more tantalizing on Friday afternoon than the aroma of simmering marinara sauce. At least, that's what Kelli used to think. She'd be cleaning her room for Sabbath when the spicy fragrance would drift down the hallway and into her room, setting her stomach to growling and luring her to the kitchen.

"What's for supper?" she'd ask.

I'd tell her. And if my meal plan didn't include the sauce she was smelling, she'd complain, "Then why am I smelling spaghetti sauce?"

"I'm making lasagna for Sabbath lunch."

She'd groan and head back to her room, her appetite for Friday night dinner temporarily ruined. Once she smelled the sauce, nothing could satisfy her craving for marinara sauce except marinara sauce. To this day, she will walk into my kitchen, smell homemade sauce, and refuse to be satisfied with anything but the sauce, and, of course, the pasta it covers.

Kelli's craving reminds me of the people Jesus talked about in Matthew 5, people who crave after righteousness, who can be satisfied with nothing less. Our Saviour said, "Blessed are they which do hunger and thirst after righteousness: for they shall be filled" (KJV).

Filled! When Kelli is finally filled with pasta and marinara sauce, she leans back in her chair, wipes the traces of tomato from her lips, and sighs with pleasure and contentment. She is truly happy!

Praise God that He is ready, able, and eager to fill you and me with the spicy sauce of righteousness—His righteousness. May we never settle for only an aroma or touch of righteousness, but may we be greedy to be totally filled with His righteousness. Therein lies true happiness.

Marinara Sauce

2 garlic cloves, minced

1 small onion

2 Tbsp. olive oil

16 oz. can tomatoes

6 oz. can tomato paste

2 tsp. basil

1½ tsp. salt

1 Tbsp. sugar (optional)

In a 2-quart saucepan over medium heat, cook the garlic and onion in oil until they are tender—about 5 minutes. Stir in the tomatoes, their liquid, and remaining ingredients. Then reduce your heat to low, cover the pan, and cook for 20 minutes or until the sauce has thickened. Don't forget to stir occasionally!

Salsa, Hot and Spicy

*"Be kind and compassionate to one another,
forgiving each other, just as in Christ God forgave you"
(Ephesians 4:32, NIV).*

I tasted my first authentic Mexican salsa at a church potluck-in-the park in southern California. The potluck was being held to welcome me to the school where I would teach grades one through four. Richard and I were newlyweds from back east, eager to make a good impression on our new church family. As I was filling my plate in the buffet line, the mother of one of my children urged me to try her famous enchiladas. Before I could respond, she dropped two on my plate. "Don't worry," she added, "my husband made me gringo-ize them."

"Gringo-ize them?" I wondered as I made my way to the table where my husband sat. Immediately, I noticed his plate held two enchiladas as well. One bite and I knew the meaning of the word "gringo-ize." I'd never tasted anything so hot in my entire life! I could only imagine how hot her "ungringo-ized" enchiladas must be. Tears coursed my cheeks as I gulped down a half a cup of lemonade in order to bravely swallow the mouthful I'd taken.

Since there was no way I would willingly put that tongue-scorching stuff in my mouth again, I looked around for an appropriate receptacle. That's when I spotted a stray dog sniffing around the picnic tables.

Checking to be certain no one was looking, I coaxed the dog to my side and scraped the remaining enchiladas from my plate to the ground. He took one whiff, sneezed, and skittered away, his tail between his legs. To hide my social "sin," I scuffed loose sand over the rejected enchiladas.

Years later, after living on the East Coast for a time, Richard and I again moved west, this time to New Mexico. While there, we grew to love Mexican food almost as much as we loved the Hispanic people. As a result, we learned a lot about chili sauce. Whether it's mild, medium, hot, or super hot, the quality of chili salsa is in its flavor. A mild salsa that lacks flavor is bland and uninteresting. A hot salsa minus flavor is just plain uncomfortable.

In the same manner, Christians' temperaments vary. Some of us are hot and spicy. We can come on too strong and bowl people over with our enthusiasm. Others are cool and smooth, so cool that they come across as aloof and uncaring.

God's cause can be damaged either way whenever the flavor of love is missing. Only the Holy Spirit can add the seasoning of love to our lives. As a result, others will see and taste the richness of God's continued presence.

Add a sprinkle of Ephesians 4:32 to your life today. "Be kind and compassionate to one another, forgiving each other, just as in Christ God forgave you." Ask the Holy Spirit to liberally sprinkle your life with grace and compassion for others.

2½ cups tomatillos, chopped
(or 2 18 oz. cans, drained and chopped)

1 medium onion, chopped

2½ Tbsp. fresh or canned jalapeño peppers, chopped

1 Tbsp. snipped cilantro

1 Tbsp. sugar (optional)

Favorite Green Salsa

[**MAKES 2 1/2 CUPS**]

Combine the tomatillos, onion, jalapeño peppers, and cilantro in a small mixing bowl (add sugar if you wish). Stir it gently; then cover and chill for one hour before serving.

1½ cups tomato (1 large)

1 small onion, chopped

¼ cup fresh or canned tomatillo, diced

1 or 2 fresh or canned jalapeño peppers, seeded and chopped

1 Tbsp. cilantro, chopped (optional)

1 clove garlic, minced

1 to 2 tsp. lime juice

¼ tsp. salt

Red Salsa

[MAKES 2 CUPS]

In a small mixing bowl, mix tomatoes, onion, tomatillos, jalapeño peppers, cilantro, garlic, lime juice, and salt. Cover and chill for one hour before serving.

Notes

BREADS

Back to Basics Wheat Bread

*"Jesus said unto them, 'I am the bread of life: he that cometh to me
shall never hunger; and he that believeth on me shall never thirst'"*
(John 6: 35, KJV).

M-m-m! There's nothing like the smell of homemade bread, cooling in the
kitchen, to trigger one's salivary glands. Before the invention of the simple plug-
in bread-maker, I would plan one entire day every two weeks to make bread. I discovered that the benefits of bread making went beyond better tasting bread and
saving money. Kneading bread was a good way to work out frustrations and a good
way for me to "bond" with my "kiddies." And, in the process, I had opportunities
to teach priceless lessons about the Bread of Life.

When the girls grew older and their spare time grew less, our bread-making days
disappeared. But the aroma of baking bread brings them back to mind as vivid as
ever.

3 to 3½ cups
all-purpose flour

3 packages active dry yeast

1¾ cups milk

¼ cup packed brown sugar

2 Tbsp. margarine or
butter

1½ tsp. salt

2 cups whole wheat flour

Basic Wheat Bread

[**M A K E S   2   L O A V E S**]

Place 2 cups of the all-purpose flour (the white stuff, not the brown stuff) into a large mixing bowl, add the yeast; then set the bowl aside.

In a small saucepan, heat the milk, brown sugar, margarine, and salt until the mixture is warm (120° to 130°) and margarine is almost melted. Stir the mixture constantly.

Next, add this warm liquid to the flour mixture in the large bowl. Set your electric mixer on low speed and beat the flour mixture for 30 seconds. When you stop, scrape the sides of the bowl with a rubber spatula. Finally, set the mixer on high and beat the mixture for 3 more minutes. The batter will be runny.

Now, stir in the whole-wheat flour (the brown stuff, not the white stuff) into the batter with a wooden spoon. Add as much of the remaining all-purpose flour as you can until the batter is no longer runny.

Using some of the remaining all-purpose flour, lightly flour a wooden board or smooth counter top. Turn the dough out onto the floured surface. If the dough sticks to your fingers, sprinkle flour on your hands before kneading.

Knead in enough of the remaining all-purpose flour to make a moderately stiff dough. It should be smooth and elastic. Knead dough for 6 to 8 minutes. This means beating and punching and twisting and folding it until you or the dough is exhausted!

Shape the dough into a ball. Then place it in a lightly greased large bowl— be sure to turn dough once to grease all of its surfaces. Cover this bowl and the dough with a dish towel and let it rise in a warm place until it doubles

(continued)

in size—usually 30 to 60 minutes. If I'm in a hurry, I will let my dough rise in my microwave oven on warm.

Now that you're rested, it's time to get violent again. Remove the dish towel and punch that dough down! Then divide it in half and cover it. Let the dough rest for 10 minutes. You should rest too!

To finish it off, shape the dough into two balls and pat each ball into a loaf shape. Place the dough in 2 greased 8 x 4 x 2" loaf pans. Cover these and let the dough rise again until nearly double—usually 30 to 60 minutes.

Finally, place the pans in your 375° oven and bake for 30 to 40 minutes. Lightly cover them with foil the last 15 minutes to prevent the crust from becoming too dark. When the bread is done, the loaf will make a hollow sound when tapped with your finger. Remove the loaves from the pans and let them cool on a wire rack before slicing.

Your home will be filled with that wonderful aroma all day!

Navajo Fry Bread

"Sir . . . we would like to see Jesus"
(John 12:21, NIV).

I met Mary at Sandia View Academy in New Mexico. She came to us from a church operated mission school for Native Americans in Arizona. She came to my class to learn English grammar, sentence structure, and literature. Since she couldn't speak English and I could speak neither Apache, her birth language; nor Navajo, her second language; I didn't know where to start. How could I share the beauty of Tennyson and Shakespeare if she didn't know the English equivalent for chair, book, or desk?

The first few days, she stared out the window, probably wishing she could be anywhere but in my class, and I prayed for wisdom. Whenever we made eye contact, I could detect a cloud of distrust in her eyes. One day after class, I asked her to stay behind. She didn't understand. I pointed to her. "You," then to the desk, "sit." She understood.

That's when we began a game of "identify the object." I would say the name of the object in English and write it on the board. And with a little coaxing, she would say the name of the object after me. After a few tries, she began to respond by saying and writing the Apache equivalent on the board beside the English spelling.

It took me a while, but finally I understood what she wanted. She wanted to teach me her language while she learned mine. Her face lighted up when I stumbled through the Apache pronunciation for classroom. My tongue seemed too big for my mouth, but I was willing to try her words as long as she worked on mine.

That night after our first session, I made a set of flashcards for her and a set for me. Months later when Mary left the academy and returned to Arizona, we both had accumulated an impressive vocabulary and a new respect for each other's cultures.

Since then, I've forgotten how to count from one to ten in Apache, but I've never forgotten Mary and the lesson on respect that she taught me. By now, I'm sure she's forgotten the crazy English teacher, her picture cards, and the words she worked so hard to teach. But I pray that sometime, somewhere along the trail of life, she remembers Jesus, the Bread of Life, whom I tried to share with her.

Navajo Fry Bread

4 cups flour

1 Tbsp. baking powder

1 tsp. salt

2 Tbsp. powdered milk

1½ cups warm water

1 cup shortening

In a large bowl, mix the flour, baking powder, salt, and powdered milk. Then mix in warm water, kneading it with hands until the dough is soft. Next, form a ball and pat it back and forth between your hands until your dough ball is flat and round.

Then you're ready to melt shortening in pan and fry the dough in hot oil. Be sure to turn it until it is brown on both sides.

Tuscany Bread

"Blessed are the meek, for they will inherit the earth"
(Matthew 5:5, NIV).

"Nothing comes from nothing . . . ," so goes a line from the musical, "The Sound of Music." The thought holds a grain of wisdom we could all afford to learn. Talents are gifts lent to us by our forefathers. What we do with them, how we develop them, becomes our gift to the next generation.

My interest in good literature came to me through my father's family. My dad loved to read. Winter evenings would find him stretched out on the sofa reading a good book. I also inherited his analytical abilities and his stick-to-it-iveness. Once he'd begun a project, he didn't rest until he saw it through to completion.

My artistic abilities came from my mother. Mama was loaded with talents. I've never met anyone else who could tinker with a musical instrument and within a few minutes play a tune. I could sketch a picture of a dress I might like to have, and she could make it, all without a pattern. She made my wedding gown from such a sketch, in one month, without a pattern and with only three fittings. That's talent.

Neither Mama nor Daddy had the benefit of a college education. But because of their encouragement, I was able to take the talents they'd given me and develop them further. And I, in turn, passed them on to my daughters. Rhonda's skills at the piano come from her grandma, not me. Kelli's vocal skills can be traced back for generations. Her sales skills, however, were definitely inherited from her daddy's line.

What a wonderful plan God had for teaching us to be grateful and to say Thank you. What a marvelously simple way to keep us from becoming self-important and from developing an inflated opinion of our persons.

The "mother" dough of Tuscany bread reminds us that we are not our own, that what we have and what we accomplish must be credited to those who came before us.

Tuscany Bread (Rustic Pané Tuscany)

[S A L T - F R E E]

First, you must make the "mother" dough. This starter dough is the basis of this unique bread.

In a small bowl, gently blend warm water with yeast. Wait 5 to 10 minutes, then add unbleached (high gluten content) flour. Mix this with your fingers for five minutes to form a loose dough. Then cover your dough with plastic wrap and set it in a warm place for 2 to 3 days.

Mix the yeast and 1/4 cup of water together, then add the rest of the water along with the "mother dough." Work the dough with your fingers until it holds together, adding the unbleached flour to form a soft ball.

Next, turn the ball out onto a floured surface (wood or marble). Knead it for 5 to 10 minutes, until it is a supple, round ball. Then coat a large mixing bowl with olive oil and place the lump of dough inside. Turn the lump of dough in the bowl until all of its surfaces are coated with oil. The oil adds flavor and keeps it from sticking.

Cover the bowl with a terry cloth towel and set it in a warm place for 2 to 3 hours or until ball doubles in size.

When it's ready, place the dough back on a floured surface. Knead it for 5 to 10 minutes; then shape into a round loaf. Gently place the unbaked loaf on a baking sheet sprinkled with cornmeal (to prevent sticking). A preheated stone slab or round piece of clay fired to withstand high heat can also be used in place of the baking sheet.

Stoneware: bake at 450° for 30 to 35 minutes.

Baking sheet: bake at 425° for 25 to 30 minutes.

Mother dough:

½ cup warm water

1 Tbsp. dry yeast

1 cup unbleached (gluten) flour

. . . .

1 Tbsp. dry yeast

¼ cup warm water

¾ cup warm water

"mother" dough

¾ cup unbleached (gluten) flour

(continued)

The bread is done when the top is brown and the loaf sounds hollow when tapped lightly.

The crust will crack as it cools, so don't let that bother you.

Serving Suggestion: Two uses for dried out Tuscany bread: "Swamp Salad" (*see recipe page 14*) and minestrone soup. To serve with minestrone soup, toast the bread; then place 1 slice in the bottom of individual soup bowls. Pour hot minestrone soup right over the bread, sprinkle with grated Romano cheese, and serve.

Christmas Breads

"Inasmuch as ye have done it unto one of the least of these . . . ye have done it unto me"
(*Matthew 25:40, KJV*).

I love Christmas—everything about Christmas! I even enjoy the jostling crowds in the malls, the tacky decorations on people's lawns, and the corny Christmas tunes—new or from years past.

Probably my favorite Christmas joy is the lights. I love the lights! I sympathize with the man in Arkansas whose neighbors took him to court to limit the number of lights on his lawn. Who cares about a little trampled grass? Bark it and join in the celebration!

I must admit, though, I do not much like the myth of Santa and his elves. To me, their magical powers come too close to imitating God's power and the work of His angels. How do you convince a child who's just learned that Santa isn't real that the stories you've been telling him about God and the angels are?

When our own daughters came along, Richard and I agreed we would not promote the Santa myth. Of course, that did not make either the girls or us popular with other children's parents who felt otherwise. More than one child went crying to Mama when they were told, "No, Virginia, there is no Santa."

Instead, we taught the girls that Christmas is a time for giving. Jesus said in

Matthew 25:40, "Inasmuch as ye have done it unto one of the least of these my brethren, ye have done it unto me." By giving to others, we give Jesus a happy birthday present.

It became a Rizzo Christmas-night tradition to make fancy breads in the shape of turtles, teddy bears, braids, and Christmas trees. Then after wrapping the cooled loaves with colored cellophane and ribbons, we'd pile into the car and deliver them to police stations, hospitals, gas stations along the interstate, and to homeless shelters—anywhere people had to work instead of being home with family and friends on Christmas Day.

We returned home tired and grateful for our blessings, taking with us the real meaning of Christmas—the privilege of giving to others, especially those who cannot return the favor. And by doing so, we give to the Creator of the universe.

Christmas Sweet Bread

[**MAKES 4 LOAVES**]

1 cup sugar

1 tsp. salt

3 packages active dry yeast

8 to 9 cups all-purpose flour

2 cups milk

1 cup butter or margarine

2 eggs

. . . .

Decorations:

frosting,
raisins,
nut pieces,
holiday sprinkles

In a large bowl, combine the sugar, salt, yeast (rehydrated), and 2 cups of flour. Then set these dry ingredients aside. In a two-quart saucepan, slowly heat milk and butter over low heat until very warm. The butter doesn't need to melt; it just needs to be soft.

With your mixer at low speed, beat in the eggs and 2 cups of flour. Then blend the warm liquid and dry ingredients. When mixed, increase your mixer speed to medium and beat for 2 minutes more.

Use a spoon to stir in enough additional flour (4 to 4½ cups) to make a soft dough. Turn the dough onto a lightly floured surface; then knead it until it is smooth (about 10 minutes), and shape it into a ball.

Place the ball of dough in a large greased bowl, turning the dough once to grease the top. Then cover it and let it rise until it doubles in size (about 1 hour). Then punch down the dough and place it onto your lightly floured surface and divide it into the number of loaves you wish to make.

Select the shape for each loaf (*see pages 58-60*). Follow the directions for each shape.

Finally, allow the bread to cool, then decorate it with frosting, raisins, nut pieces, and holiday sprinkles. Merry Christmas!

¼ sweet dough recipe

1 egg

Water

. . . .

Decorations:
raisins or currants,
multicolored sprinkles

. . . .

Sugar glaze:

In a small bowl, stir
½ cup confectioner's
sugar and 2 to 3 tsp.
water until smooth.

Dough Shapes—Turtle
[MAKES 4 TURTLES]

Prepare the sweet dough as outlined. Divide it into four equal parts and shape those into four balls. Cover the dough balls and set three aside.

First, the turtle body. Take one ball and cut off a 1/2 cup piece from the dough. Set this aside and shape the remaining piece into a rope. Spiral the rope into a mound and place it on a cookie sheet.

Next, roll the reserved piece into a rope also. Cut a two-inch piece of the rope and shape it into the oval ball for the turtle's head. Cut four smaller pieces and shape those into feet. Shape a snippet of dough for the tail. Then tuck the head, legs, and tail under the oval ball body to seal. Raisins or currants make good turtle eyes. Do the same with the other three balls of dough.

Finally, beat an egg into a little water. Brush this mixture on your turtles. Let them rise until they double in size; then bake them in preheated oven at 375° for 20 to 30 minutes. Decorate your baked turtles with sugar glaze and multicolored sprinkles.

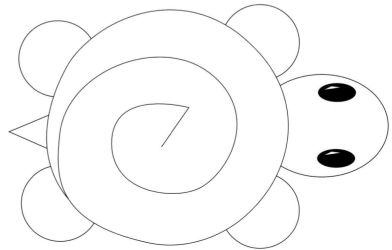

Dough Shapes—Teddy Bear
[MAKES 4 TEDDY BEARS]

¼ sweet dough recipe

1 egg

water

. . . .

Decorations:

raisins,
chocolate chips,
M&Ms,
multicolored sprinkles

. . . .

Sugar glaze:

In a small bowl, stir
½ cup confectioner's
sugar and 2 to 3 tsp.
water until smooth.

Prepare the sweet dough as outlined. Divide it into four equal parts and shape those into four balls. Cover the dough balls and set three aside.

First, take one ball and cut off a cup-size piece of dough to set aside. Shape the remaining dough into an oval ball and place it on a cookie sheet. Take the cup-size piece of dough you set aside and divide it into seven pieces, one piece being larger than the other six. Roll the six pieces into six balls.

Break off a small piece from the largest mound of dough and set it aside. Mold the larger piece of dough into a circle for teddy's head. Attach it to his body. Flatten two of the smaller balls and place one on each side of the head for ears. Roll the small piece of dough you broke off into a ball and flatten it onto teddy's face for his muzzle. Stick a raisin into it for his nose. Attach two of the remaining balls for legs and two for arms. Use raisins, chocolate chips, or M&Ms for eyes, nose and buttons on his jacket. Do the same with the other three original balls to make four teddy bears.

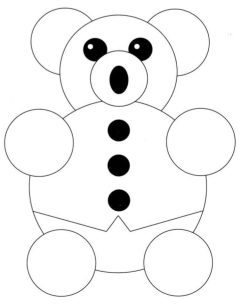

Finally, beat an egg into a little water. Brush this mixture on the teddy bears. Let them rise until they double in size, then bake them in preheated oven at 375° for 20 to 30 minutes. Decorate your baked teddy bears with sugar glaze and multicolored sprinkles.

1/4 sweet dough recipe

1 egg

water

· · · · · · · · · · ·

Decorations:

multicolored sprinkles, wedding cake balls

· · · · · · · · · · ·

Sugar glaze:

In a small bowl, stir ½ cup confectioner's sugar and 2 to 3 tsp. water until smooth.

Dough Shapes—Tree
[MAKES 4 TREES]

Prepare the sweet dough as outlined. Divide it into four equal parts and shape those into four balls. Cover the dough balls and set three aside.

For each tree, divide one of the balls into 16 small balls. Arrange those balls on a cookie sheet in the following pattern:

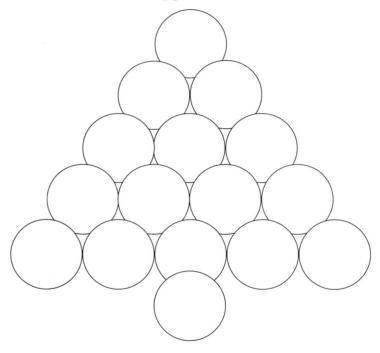

Finally, beat an egg into a little water. Brush this mixture on the trees. Let them rise until they double in size; then bake them in preheated oven at 375° for 20 to 30 minutes. Decorate your baked trees with sugar glaze, multicolored sprinkles, and silver wedding cake balls.

Apple-filled Bran Muffins

"I am the vine, ye are the branches"
(John 15:5, KJV).

When we lived in Pennsylvania, we had an apple tree in our backyard. The tree produced two distinct kinds of apples—one, red-skinned and sweet but a bit mealy; the other, green-skinned, tart and crisp. The stock producing the green apple had been grafted onto the tree years earlier. Combining the fruit produced the best apple sauce you could ever want to taste.

It kind of makes me think of John 15:1-4 where Jesus says, "I am the true vine. . . . As the branch cannot bear fruit of itself . . . . Neither can you, unless you abide in me" (NKJV). The two apples, together and attached to the same tree, became more delicious than if they had been separate from each other.

You and I are often too tart or too mushy by ourselves, but when blended with our brothers and sisters in Christ and united by the Source of true love, we can produce a flavorful blend that is pleasing to the Creator and to His service.

1/3 cup chopped apple

1/4 cup chopped walnuts

2 Tbsp. brown sugar

1 Tbsp. softened margarine

1/2 tsp. ground cinnamon

1 1/4 cups all-purpose flour

1/4 cup granulated sugar

1 Tbsp. baking powder

1/4 tsp. salt

1 cup whole bran cereal

1 cup milk

1 beaten egg

2 Tbsp. cooking oil

Apple-filled Bran Muffins
[**MAKES 12 MUFFINS**]

In a small bowl, stir together the apple, nuts, brown sugar, margarine, and cinnamon; then set it aside. In a large mixing bowl, stir together the flour, sugar, baking powder, and salt. Finally, in a medium mixing bowl (I hope you're not running out of bowls!), stir together the cereal and milk. Let it stand for five minutes; then add the egg and oil and stir it all again.

Now add the cereal mixture (medium bowl!) to the dry ingredients (large bowl!). Stir it until the cereal is moistened. Spoon about half of this batter into your twelve lined or greased muffin cups, leaving each one half full. Plop a rounded teaspoonful of the apple filling (small bowl!) into each muffin cup. Then add the remaining batter to fill them up. Bake the muffins at 400° for 20 minutes or until the tops are golden. Serve 'em warm!

Apricot Bread

"The way of a fool seems right to him"
(Proverbs 12:15, NIV).

I never look an apricot in the pit without remembering my visit to Capitol Reef National Park and Rhonda's pair of new sneakers. New, but ugly. An uglier pair of sneakers you will never find! They were parrot green with orange swooshes. Yes, you read right—green and orange.

We'd traveled from Oregon to Utah to spend the weekend camping with family members from Arkansas. While there was plenty of room inside our travel trailer, Rhonda and Kelli opted to sleep in a pup tent one night.

Now, understand, I enjoy camping. That is, until I have to get out of my comfy bed in the middle of the night and hoof it to the gray cement block building.

I'd barely locked the door to my stall when someone entered the stall next to me. I glanced down and spotted parrot green tennies with orange swooshes on the sides. Rhonda! Aha! What an advantage! I knew she was there, but she didn't know I was there, if that makes any sense. What an opportunity!

You see, I'm an incorrigible tease. When I'm on a roll, even my patient sheltie collie, Corky, will get up and walk to the other side of the room to keep my incessant teasing from interrupting her sleep.

Snatching the opportunity to unnerve Rhonda, I tore a few sheets of toilet paper into little pieces and rolled them into pebble-sized balls. I flicked one over the wall and waited.

Silence.

I flicked two over the wall, then three. Still silence. This is ridiculous, I thought. I'm not going to wait around all night for her to realize I'm here. So I took the entire handful of toilet paper pebbles and threw them over the wall.

The night air throbbed with silence. Silence?

Tired of not getting a reaction, I stretched my foot under the divider and stomped on the sneaker closest to me. She slid it to the far side of the stall.

Then it hit me. No. No! Impossible. There couldn't be two people in the same remote campground wearing identical sneakers, especially ugly green ones with orange swooshes. Could there?

Oh no, I groaned to myself, how could I be so stupid? I started to giggle.

The woman in the next stall exited to the sink while I giggled louder. Now I had another problem; once I start giggling, I can't stop.

Between giggles, I realized I had to try to explain why I was assaulting a stranger with toilet paper pebbles in the middle of the night, and worse yet, why I accosted her sneaker.

I rushed out of the stall and caught the terrified woman drying her hands by the sink. She stared at me with the panicked look of a deer caught in the headlights of an oncoming automobile. I tried to explain, but my words broke down with uncontrollable laughter.

Tears streamed down my face. I doubled over, clutching my stomach. She spied her chance for escape, rushed past me, and disappeared into the night.

The next morning, who should I meet coming out from the restroom while I was heading in, but the woman with the green and orange sneakers. She took one look at me and dashed in the opposite direction. I've never seen an 80-year-old woman run so fast in my life!

Even now, as I repeat this story to audiences everywhere—it is requested at almost every women's retreat I attend—I have to say I was certain it was Rhonda in the next stall. Before I threw the first toilet paper pebble, I was convinced it was my daughter. Yet, all my certainty didn't change the fact I was wrong, dead wrong. I'd played the part of a fool.

Did I learn a lesson from the experience? Perhaps. I try to check my facts before I do something too stupid.

You have a right to ask, "What does the sneaker story have to do with apricots?" The connection that triggers my memory of my faux pas is the apricot trees near Capitol Reef National Park. They produce the sweetest apricots you ever tasted. We stuffed ourselves with apricots during our stay; then before we left, we loaded the back window of our automobile with the scrumptious fruit and let them sun-dry during our ride home. Of course, most of the apricots never made it home. We munched them all the way across Utah, Nevada, and California.

16 oz. can apricot halves, drained

1¾ cups all-purpose flour

¾ cup whole wheat flour

1¼ cups sugar

3½ tsp. baking powder

1 tsp. salt

½ tsp. pumpkin-pie spice

2 beaten eggs

½ cup milk

3 Tbsp. cooking oil

1 cup dried apricots, diced

Apricot Bread

[**MAKES 2 LOAVES**]

In a blender, blend the canned apricots until they are smooth; then set them aside. In a large bowl, combine the all-purpose flour, whole wheat flour, sugar, baking powder, salt and pumpkin-pie spice. In another bowl, combine the eggs, the apricot puree, the milk, and the oil.

Stir this mixture into the flour mixture until the whole batch is moist. Now add your blended dried apricots and stir lightly.

Pour it all into 2 greased 8 x 4 x 2" loaf pans, then bake it at 350° for 45 to 50 minutes. Remove the bread from the pans and allow it to cool completely before serving.

Pennsylvania Johnnycake

"I was young and now I am old, yet I have never seen the righteous forsaken
or their children begging bread"
(Psalm 37: 25, NIV).

My father lost his job when he gave his heart to God. He'd been working for his brother, a general contractor. When Daddy told Uncle Bill that he planned to be baptized, my uncle fired him and disowned him as a brother. The loss went far beyond the financial, for my father had always been very close to his family. Fortunately, Uncle Bill couldn't take away the skills my father had learned from him.

My dad set up his own contracting business. The first few years were lean, as any entrepreneur will tell you. Not only was my father starting from scratch, but he had to combat my uncle's bad publicity. He was well-known in the area, and he never missed an opportunity to besmirch my father's skills and his reputation.

During that time, I remember praying that "The Millionaire," from a television program of the same name, would knock on our door. God listened, and I believe, smiled, at the five-year-old's prayer that day.

And He answered it! Not with a million-dollar check (I wouldn't know what a million dollars looked like today, let alone when I was five), but with security— what I really wanted, in my heart of hearts. God kept His word. I never went hungry. I never had to beg for my bread.

Some suppers consisted of white bread and milk. A variation on the bread that I always enjoyed was corn bread, or "johnnycake" as we called it. I didn't learn until years later that the term *"johnnycake"* came from "journeycake," a corn bread carried by early American hunters and traders.

Another fact I discovered is that every region of the country has its own variation on johnnycake. And while I seldom eat a bowl of white bread and milk today, I do enjoy a good bowl of hot johnnycake with ice-cold milk poured over the top.

Pennsylvania Johnnycake

1 egg

¼ cup all-purpose flour

1 cup + 2 Tbsp. milk

1¼ cups cornmeal

3 Tbsp. soft shortening

2 Tbsp. sugar

3 tsp. baking powder

1 tsp. salt

Preheat your oven to 450°. Grease a square pan (9 x 9 x 1¾") and let it warm in the oven while you mix the batter.

First, beat the egg. Measure the flour by the dip-level-pour method. Beat in rest of the ingredients, just until the batter is smooth. Then spoon the batter into your warm pan and bake for 20 to 25 minutes.

Cut the corn bread into squares to serve. To eat it the way I like it, break a piece into a cereal bowl and pour milk over the top. Once in a while, try adding a little honey.

Sandwiches

"Even the very hairs of your head are all numbered.
So don't be afraid; you are worth more than many sparrows"
(Matthew 10:30, NIV).

To me, the sandwich is sacred. I love 'em! There is something so satisfying about biting into a thick and messy lettuce-and-tomato sandwich. Or dunking a peanut-butter-and-pomegranate-jelly sandwich in a tall, frosty glass of milk. Or inhaling the delicious aroma of a freshly made toasted cheese sandwich. Where would I be without sandwiches?

Created in 1762, the sandwich was probably the first example of the modern phenomena of "fast food," a meal on the fly. And it bears the name of its inventor to this day.

The scoundrel John Montague, the fourth earl of Sandwich, was a notoriously corrupt gambler. He thought nothing of betraying family members and friends. The legend says that since Montague could not be interrupted for something like a meal during a 24-hour card game, Montague's valet brought him sliced beef between bread—hence the first sandwich.

Of course, this shows how unfair life can be—no one knows the name of the valet who actually created the sandwich.

There are other nobodys who made their mark in history. Eli Whitney, the famed father of the cotton gin, was rumored to have taken the credit from one of his slaves. Who is the nobody who invented the first wheel? The first dugout canoe? The first kite?

With God there are no nobodys. He know the name of each of us and everything about us. He knows how many gray hairs I have on my head. He knows how many gray thoughts I have in my mind. Through the blood of Jesus Christ, my name is written in the book of life.

While I've included the story for its trivia and not so trivial value, like it or not, sandwiches are a permanent part of our lives. For that reason, I've included four unusual and interesting sandwiches, two from the Middle East and two from Italy.

1 cup bulgar wheat

1 cup boiling water

1 can of vegetarian burger

½ cup minced onion

1 egg, lightly beaten

½ cup fresh parsley,
coarsely chopped

½ tsp. salt

½ tsp. cumin, ground

6 whole wheat pita breads

. . . .

Dressing:

1 cup plain yogurt
(low fat)

3 medium tomatoes,
minced

2 Tbsp. fresh dill, chopped

Arabian Flatbread Sandwich

[**MAKES 6 SANDWICHES**]

Heat your oven to 350° while you lightly grease a 15½ x 10 x 1" baking dish. In a large bowl, combine the bulgar with water and let it stand until the water is absorbed (about 30 minutes). Then fluff it with a fork and add burger, onion, egg, parsley, salt, and cumin. Mix it all lightly until combined.

Shape the mixture into meatballs. Place the meatballs on metal or wooden skewers (three meatballs to a skewer) and soak them in water for ten minutes. Place the skewers on your prepared baking sheet and bake for 20 minutes or until the meatballs are browned, turning them occasionally.

Meanwhile, in a small bowl, combine the yogurt, tomato, and dill. Serve by rolling pita bread tightly around each skewer and removing the skewered meatballs. Drizzle a generous amount of the yogurt dressing onto the meatballs.

Falafel Burgers

1 box falafel mix (7.4 oz.)

½ cup cherry tomatoes, halved

½ cup radish sprouts

½ cup cucumber, diced and seeded

½ cup plain yogurt, low fat

½ cup sesame tehini (smooth paste)

¼ cup water

3 Tbsp. lemon juice, fresh

1 cup olive oil

4 whole wheat pita breads, warmed

Prepare the falafel mix according to directions on the box. Shape the dough into four equal-sized patties. Combine the tomatoes, sprouts, and cucumber in a small bowl; then whisk together the yogurt, tahini, water, and lemon juice in a second small bowl. Chill the sauce and the vegetable mixture while you cook the burgers.

In a large skillet, heat some oil to a sizzle. Fry your patties until they are golden and crispy on both sides (about 5 minutes). Drain each on a paper towel.

To serve, cut a small portion off the pita bread, then place the falafel burger inside the pocket. Place the vegetable mixture inside next; then drizzle tahini sauce over the top.

⅔ cup olive oil

¼ cup red wine vinegar
(optional)

2 tsp. Italian seasoning

1 tsp. fennel seeds,
crushed

1 tsp. salt (optional)

1 medium eggplant,
cut into one-inch chunks
(about four cups)

2 large plum tomatoes,
halved

1 jar roasted red peppers,
(7-inch size) cut into
one-inch chunks,
drained and patted dry

1 medium zucchini, cut
into one-inch chunks
(2 cups)

1 loaf French or Italian
bread (16 inches long),
split and toasted

1 cup mozzarella cheese

Italian Ratatouille Sub

[**MAKES 4 SANDWICHES**]

In a small bowl, blend together the oil, vinegar, Italian seasoning, fennel seeds, and salt.

Sauté the eggplant, tomatoes, and roasted peppers in 2 teaspoons of the dressing until the eggplant is tender (10 minutes). Then add zucchini and sauté the mixture for two more minutes.

To serve, pour 1/3 cup of the herb dressing over the toasted bread. Spoon the hot vegetables on the bottom half of bread, sprinkle with cheese; then drizzle the remaining dressing over that. Serve with black olives, jalapeño peppers, and green onions on the side.

16 oz. bag frozen
mixed vegetables, defrosted

15 oz. can chick peas,
rinsed and drained

⅓ cup low-calorie
Italian salad dressing

¼ cup frozen apple juice
concentrate, defrosted

1 Tbsp. olive oil

2 Tbsp. rice or
white wine vinegar

2 Tbsp. fresh lemon juice

2 cloves minced garlic, or
¼ tsp. powdered garlic

8 leaves lettuce,
rinsed and dried

8 pita breads

sesame seeds (optional)

Italian Veggie Sandwich
[MAKES 8 SERVINGS]

Combine the frozen vegetables and chick peas in a bowl. Then in a jar with a tight fitting lid, shake the salad dressing, juice concentrate, oil, vinegar, lemon juice, and garlic to mix well. Pour this over the vegetable mixture and marinate for a few hours in the refrigerator.

To serve, cut one end off the pita breads and arrange one lettuce leaf inside each pita pocket. Then stuff each pita pocket with 1/2 cup of the vegetable mixture and sprinkle it with sesame seeds. Serve chilled and enjoy!

Notes

VEGETABLE SIDE DISHES

Acorn Squash With Applesauce

"All the believers were one in heart and mind. . . .
they shared everything they had"
(Acts 4:32, NIV).

On a crisp autumn day, the young mothers on the Blue Mountain Academy staff converged on my giant kitchen to make applesauce while our preschoolers played in the backyard. I don't know what was more fun; the picking, the peeling, the "saucing," or the chatter!

I do know that a task that usually requires hours of labor was finished in a short time. And at the end of the afternoon, each of us had several quarts of applesauce to show for it.

Even though we lived in close proximity, the stay-at-home wives and mothers on a busy academy campus had little time to get together with one another. There was the occasional shopping trip or church potluck, but mostly we enjoyed the company of our little ones and supplied support for our teacher husbands.

That one day, it was as if we'd turned back the clock to our great-grandmothers' days of quilting bees, barn raisings, and corn huskings. We were unified in goal and purpose. As a result, we enjoyed the labors of that day and the bounty of those apple trees throughout the winter. And from our time together, we received a kinder, gentler understanding of one another.

2 medium acorn squash

3 cups applesauce
(*see recipe opposite*)

¼ tsp. ground nutmeg

¼ tsp. ground cinnamon

¼ tsp. salt

2 Tsp. margarine
(optional)

Acorn Squash With Applesauce

Halve squash lengthwise, then remove and discard seeds. Place squash, cut-side down, in a microwavable baking dish—12 x 7½ x 2". With the dish uncovered, microwave on 100% power (high) for 13 to 16 minutes or till tender, giving the dish a half-turn once.

In the meantime, combine the apple, nutmeg, and salt in a small bowl.

Remove the dish from the microwave and turn the squash halves over. Spoon the applesauce mixture into the squash cavities. Dot with margarine.

Cover with wax paper; then microwave for 5 to 7 minutes or until the fruit is hot. Sprinkle the dish with cinnamon or nutmeg, if you desire.

Applesauce

4 medium cooking apples
(peeled and quartered
as you like them)

¼ to ½ cup sugar

½ cup water

½ tsp. cinnamon

Combine the apples and water in a 2½-quart casserole dish. Cover and microwave for 7 to 9 minutes (until fruit is soft, but not mushy).

Add sugar until you like the taste. Press the applesauce through a colander, if you wish. Season with cinnamon, if you like!

Artichoke a la Lemon-butter Sauce

"Taste and see that the Lord is good"
(Psalm 34:7, KJV).

The first time I tasted an artichoke, I was visiting my future in-law's home in New York City. When the family discovered I'd never before eaten one, they educated me on the proper techniques for eating the succulent thistle.

My first reaction to artichoke was less than ecstatic. I didn't hate it, but I certainly wouldn't have walked across the street for one. I was fascinated to learn that when you eat the meat from an artichoke leaf, then drink water, you will taste licorice. But if you drink milk instead, it will taste sweet in your mouth.

By the time Richard and I married, I'd developed a love for the prickly fruit. We ate it as often as we could afford it. When our daughters came along, artichokes were as common on our dinner table as peas and corn on other American children's tables. However, as much as Rhonda and Kelli enjoyed their individual artichokes, they decided they didn't like the heart. They wouldn't eat it no matter how much we told them that the heart was the best part. As a result, every time we served artichokes, Richard and I enjoyed two artichoke hearts instead of only one choke.

I remember the day Rhonda first discovered the heart's rich flavor. "Hey," she exclaimed in surprise, "why didn't you tell me this was so good?"

"Haven't you been listening? We tried. Don't you remember?" her father answered.

King David wrote in Psalm 34:8, "Taste and see that the Lord is good." Too bad so many of God's children miss out on the full rich flavor of God's abundant love because of preconceived ideas about God and His salvation.

"Father, I don't want to miss out on a thing You have to offer. Make me greedy, Lord, for the taste of salvation and for the sight of Your loving goodness."

artichokes,
French globe type
(one per serving)

. . . .

Lemon-butter sauce:

lemon, (one per serving)

butter or margarine, melted
(1 Tbsp. per serving)

salt to taste

Artichoke a la Lemon-butter Sauce

[**MAKES AS MANY SERVINGS AS YOU NEED**]

Cut one inch off the top of the artichoke with a sharp knife. Then trim the stem until only a 1/2" stub remains. Next, remove the outside lower leaves and cut off thorny leaf tips.

Boil the artichoke for 20 to 45 minutes or until leaf pulls away easily.

My favorite way to serve artichoke is to place one "choke" per person on a salad plate and offer small individual dishes for lemon-butter dip. Speaking of the lemon-butter dip . . .

Squeeze all the juice from one lemon into a teacup. Then add 1 tablespoon of butter or margarine and salt to taste. Melt the butter over low heat, stirring to blend all the elements.

Graceful Artichoke Dining: To eat an artichoke gracefully, pull off a leaf and dip the wide end into the lemon-butter sauce. Then pull the leaf between your teeth to scrape off the soft pulp. Toss the remains. When all the leaves have been eaten, use a knife and fork to cut off and discard the fuzzy "choke," or core. Then comes my favorite part! Cut the remaining artichoke heart into dip-sized pieces, dip each piece into the lemon-butter sauce, and enjoy!

Stuffed Mushrooms

"I am the way and the truth and the life"
(John 14:6, NIV).

In Oregon, mushrooms grow in abundance. Flat ones, umbrella ones, leggy ones—they dot people's lawns for most of the year. And in amazing abundance, huge, tiny, round, and skinny mushrooms can be found scattered atop the fern-strewn forest floor.

We have friends who loved to go mushrooming, especially for the delicate flavored morels. They invited us along on several of their forays, but we always declined. Knowing what we know about mushrooms, we were sure our baskets would be filled with the deadly poisonous kinds—death angels.

We loved our friends, but we didn't completely trust their detective skills. I wanted to please my friends by going along, but I just couldn't do it. I preferred to save my Epicurean appetite for mushrooms for the supermarket variety. I suppose with my twisted reasoning, I figured that if I ate a poisonous mushroom purchased at the market, at least, my children could file a wrongful-death suit.

We all have our own "mushroom story," things we don't trust doing despite the urging of friends or family members. My salvation is one of those things I choose to place in the hands of my Saviour instead of in the hearsay and theories of friends, family, or other amateur theologians.

Jesus said, "I am the way and the truth and the life." He is my only source of salvation, and His Word, the only source of truth.

When people ask me, "What if you're wrong? What if salvation isn't quite so simple?"—and they do—I say, "If I'm wrong, then God's promises are wrong, and on the judgment day, He'll have the explaining to do, not me."

18 large mushrooms

1 Tbsp. olive oil

¼ cup minced onion

1 clove minced garlic

¼ cup walnuts,
finely chopped

1 shredded wheat biscuit,
crushed

1 Tbsp. grated Parmesan
cheese

½ tsp. "Herb Seasoning"
(*see recipe next*)

½ tsp. paprika (optional)

Stuffed Mushrooms

[**MAKES 6 SERVINGS**]

Preheat your oven to 350°. Clean your mushrooms; then remove and chop the stems.

Heat oil in a skillet with a nonstick surface and sauté the mushroom stems, onion, garlic, and walnuts for 4 to 5 minutes. Remove the skillet from the heat and stir in shredded wheat, Parmesan cheese, and herb seasoning.

Stuff the mushroom caps with your mixture. Place the mushrooms in a shallow baking dish and sprinkle them with paprika. Then bake them for 20 to 25 minutes until mushrooms are tender.

Herb Seasoning

1 Tbsp. garlic powder

1 tsp. each:

basil
mace
marjoram
onion powder
parsley
sage
savory
thyme

½ tsp. cayenne pepper

Combine all the ingredients in a small bowl. Toss them gently until they are well blended; then store the seasoning in an airtight container. This seasoning can be stored in a cool, dark place for up to six months.

Yummy Green Beans

"My God will meet all your needs
according to his glorious riches in Christ Jesus"
(Philippians 4:19, NIV).

What Wisconsin lacks in mountain scenery, it more than makes up for in its rich soil and friendly people. During our three-year stint there, I discovered the value of both. We lived next-door to an avid gardener, Grant Guth, and his beautiful wife, Helen.

Weeds met their match in Grant. He maintained a vegetable garden that could feed the population of most third-world countries. Even on an August evening when the mosquitoes waxed monstrous and cagey, I would see Grant, clothed in a beekeeper's suit, hood and all, caring for his garden.

When the green beans came on, my telephone would ring. It would be Helen proposing she and I have a bean-freezing bee at her house. We'd sit around her Formica-topped kitchen table, popping beans as we talked. I returned home at the end of the afternoon with more than a dozen bags of green beans to show for my efforts. The woman had a wealth of wisdom. And as a young mother, I could use all I could get.

Over the years, I forgot how pleasant and rich were our times together until recently. I was listening to a Christian radio presentation on family life. The speaker was explaining why women expect so much from their spouses. Part of the reason is, the female emotional support system their grandmothers enjoyed is no longer available. Families extended to aunts, cousins, nieces, and grandmas, all with wise—and sometimes not-so-wise—advice.

Today, women, most of whom are employed outside the home, have neither time nor energy for female socializing. Even the coffee-klatches of our mother's day no longer exist. So, we turn to our husbands to supply the missing ingredients in our lives.

Unfortunately, their roles and their support systems have also changed over the years. They struggle to make sense out of their lives as well, wondering why they can't be all things to the woman they married.

Imagine—God saw our needs before we did! He planted seeds in the hearts of a few of His faithful children. The result? The seeds have blossomed into the emergence of women's and men's ministries.

How strange to remember Mrs. Guth and realize she was a woman before her time, or perhaps, after her time. I am thankful to her for taking one inexperienced and homesick young mother and giving her the support she needed over a colander of fresh green beans.

2 lb. fresh cut green beans

2 Tbsp. onions, chopped

4 Tbsp. olive oil

2 Tbsp. fresh parsley,
minced

1 clove garlic, chopped

½ tsp. sugar

1 tsp. dill weed, basil,
or thyme

1 lemon

Mama's Green Beans

Snap off the ends of the green beans, then cut them crosswise into 1" lengths. Boil them in salted water for 15 to 20 minutes; then drain off the water.

Next, heat oil in a skillet. Add garlic, herb, onions, parsley, and sugar. Pour this mixture over the beans and toss away! Reheat the beans slowly; then serve with lemon wedges.

Potato Toppers

"Let us hold firmly to the faith we profess"
(Hebrews 4:14b, NIV).

An ancient Irish blessing says, "May you always be eating one potato, peeling a second, have a third in your fist, and your eye on a fourth." Whether mashed, sliced, fried, chipped, hashed, scalloped, microwaved, or baked, the humble potato is well-loved. For millions of Americans, potatoes are a basic staple, and perhaps, because it will keep for so long in a dry, dark place, the most inexpensive, available and versatile of vegetables.

Potatoes are a lot like faith, a basic staple of Christianity. Without faith in God, the diet of religion would be unsatisfying. A dynamic faith infuses men and women with power to do the incredible. Faith opens heaven's storehouse of blessings. It is versatile, suitable for every occasion, inexpensive, since it is first a gift to us from the heavenly Father.

Unlike the lowly potato, faith thrives in dark places, light places, hot or cold, and becomes evident in adversity. Yes, faith is as much a necessity to the Christian's spiritual diet as potatoes are to the American diet.

William Shakespeare wrote, "Let it rain potatoes." Perhaps we should be praying, "Let it rain faith."

Side dish or main course, the following baked potato toppers will add new zest to an old favorite.

Santa Fe Toppers

¾ cup tomato sauce

½ cup salsa

1 cup cubed soy chicken
or tofu

8 oz. can drained
whole-kernel corn

¼ cup green onion,
thinly sliced

½ cup shredded cheese,
Colby or Monterey Jack

½ cup green
chili peppers, diced

4 large baked potatoes

In a quart saucepan, combine the tomato sauce and salsa and bring it to a boil. In a second saucepan, combine the soy chicken or tofu and the corn and green onion. Heat this but don't boil.

Spoon the chicken/corn mixture atop split baked potatoes. Top with sauce, cheese, and green chili peppers.

Garden Topper

1 Tbsp. margarine or butter

2 medium zucchini, thinly sliced

1 cup fresh mushrooms, sliced

¼ cup red onion wedges, thin

1 tsp. salt

8 oz. of plain yogurt, low-fat

1 Tbsp. fresh thyme or savory

1 Tbsp. fresh parsley, snipped

½ tsp. celery seed

4 large baked potatoes

Melt your margarine or butter in small skillet. Add the zucchini, fresh mushrooms, onions, and salt. Cook it all uncovered until the onion is tender (not brown) and liquid has evaporated.

Stir the yogurt and herbs together. Then split the potatoes and spoon the yogurt mixture onto the potatoes. Top it off with the vegetable mixture and serve.

Quickie Topper
[**MAKES 2 SERVINGS**]

2 large potatoes

1 can Progresso lentil soup

½ cup grated cheese

Prepare the potatoes for microwaving by puncturing the skins with the point of a knife or fork tines. Microwave the potatoes 4 to 7 minutes (time will vary depending on your microwave and the size of your potatoes). In a small saucepan, heat the lentil soup to boiling.

When the potatoes are done, split them open and pour on the lentil soup. Sprinkle with grated cheese and serve.

Notes

Angel-Hair Pasta With Artichoke Hearts

*"Jesus . . . came to a village where a woman
named Martha opened her home to him"
(Luke 10:38, NIV).*

Have you ever wished you were more "Martha" than "Mary?"

You remember the story of Jesus visiting His friends in Bethany. While Martha prepared the food for a party of fifteen, Mary sat at the feet of Jesus. I confess, I am more often Mary than Martha. I don't function well in another woman's kitchen, and I get all stressed out when I anticipate serving guests in my own home.

I picture Martha as the kind of hostess who spent hours creating those fancy canapés, who served delicate little watercress sandwiches with their crusts removed, who delights in making her own pasta and stuffing her own cannolis. Her kitchen looks like a page from *Better Homes and Gardens*. Her parlor looks like a photo in *Architectural Digest*. And her bathroom looks like Laura Ashley breezed through. That's for expected guests.

For unexpected guests, my "Martha" is always prepared, whether it be a party of two or twenty. I admit that, for me, unexpected guests are easier on my nerves. I figure if a person drops in unannounced or calls at the last minute, he or she expects to see a little disorganization in my organization. Besides, I don't have to worry about how tall the male guests are so as to know whether or not I should scrub the top of the refrigerator before they arrive.

Family and close friends are something totally different. I like having them drop by any old time. (Oh yes, once my guests arrive, planned or otherwise, I relax and have a great time anyway. It's the anticipation that kills me.)

My daughter Rhonda created the following quickie nonrecipe that looks great and tastes so good I serve it to planned and unplanned guests alike. Add a tossed salad, breadsticks, apple juice, and great conversation, and you have the recipe for a good time.

Now, I can honestly say, "Mi casa es su casa," or "My house is your house." Drop by anytime. I can always throw more pasta in the pot.

Angel-Hair Pasta With Artichoke Hearts

8 oz. package of
angel-hair pasta

6 artichoke hearts
per person

salt and pepper (optional)

garlic powder to taste

powdered Parmesan or
Romano cheese to taste

Cook the angel-hair noodles in boiling water; then drain them (I know, you already knew that, but recipes are supposed to give every step). In a large bowl, mix all of the ingredients. Then garnish with a dusting of the powdered cheese and serve! The entire meal takes less than ten minutes to prepare.

Adventure Casserole

I love adventures! I love exploring the "road less traveled." As a young child, when other kids played "cowboys and Indians," my backyard became a mission field, complete with roaring lions, renegade tigers, rogue elephants, and poisonous snakes. When I mastered the art of reading, I read every book I could find on India. By third grade, I knew all the country's governmental statistics, imports, exports, and population divisions. I knew that someday I would be a missionary to India.

I grew up, graduated from high school, went to college, and met an outrageously brilliant young man from New York City. When I told Richard of my dream, he stared in disbelief. His dream was to graduate from college, get his master's degree, get a job in Westchester County, north of the city, have kids, and buy a house, a station wagon, and a dog. This wacky girl just didn't fit his plans.

Fortunately, we both wanted to follow God's plans for our lives. Our adventure began the day after our wedding in upstate New York, when we climbed into our '57 Chevy, loaded with all our earthly possessions, and headed west for California. While I never did make it to India, our adventure has taken us to Pennsylvania,

Virginia, New Mexico, Oregon, and back to California.

Recently, our younger daughter, Kelli, and her husband, Mark, announced an adventure toward which they believe God is directing them. They have decided to dedicate their lives to a full-time mission. Not one where there's a paycheck at the end of the month, but one where every day is a faith adventure in Christ Jesus. One of the places in which they will "mission" is India.

For me to go is one thing, but for my precious daughter to risk everything gives me cause to pause. Just how strong is my faith, after all? Playing at faith is easy. Many of us do it regularly. But living by faith is the real thing.

My Jesus said, "Go ye into all the world"—go in My name and believe. That same Jesus is filling Kelli and Mark with His Spirit of adventure—not a spirit of curiosity, but of faith. It's an important lesson to learn from one's children.

"Lord, fill me with Your Spirit of adventure. Teach me to trust You to lead me wherever You would have me go."

For those of you who crave a bit of adventure, have fun with the following recipe while you're learning to trust on the Lord.

Adventure Casserole

[MAKES 3-6 SERVINGS]

1 cup main ingredient

1 cup second ingredient

1 to 2 cups starchy ingredient

1½ cups binder

¼ cup of a garnish

seasoning

topping

Choose a main ingredient. It can be whatever you're in the mood for—soy meat, burger, or a vegetable. Place in large mixing bowl. Now choose a second ingredient—chopped celery, mushrooms, hard-boiled eggs, frozen peas, maybe even a second cup of whatever you chose as a main ingredient—and add it in.

Add 1 to 2 cups of a starchy ingredient. Take your pick—crushed potato chips, croutons, bread crumbs, cooked noodles, or rice. Add 1½ cups of something that will bind it together. Try mayonnaise, cream sauce, sour cream, plain yogurt, or a cream-soup base. Add 1/4 cup of a garnish such as pimento, olive pieces, chopped nuts, or capers. Add some seasoning—maybe one or two tablespoons of lemon juice, soy sauce, or Worchester sauce; maybe one-quarter cup of chopped onion or a minced clove of garlic; maybe two teaspoons of curry powder or more grated cheese.

Mix everything together. If it seems too dry, add 1/4 to 1/2 cup of milk or vegetable broth. Then pour it into a buttered casserole dish. Spread a topping—buttered bread crumbs, chopped nuts, grated cheese, crushed potato chips, or Chinese noodles—over the mixture. Bake it at 350° for 30 to 45 minutes.

Try some new combinations each time. You won't be creating just a meal—it'll be an adventure!

Barley Casserole

"The poor will eat and be satisfied;
they who seek the Lord will praise him"
(Psalm 22:26, NIV).

I would have loved to have been there the day Jesus took the little boy's lunch, blessed it, then multiplied it for the thousands of people gathered on that grassy hillside. Imagine watching the Creator hand out piece after piece after piece, to the crowd's astonishment. Can't you hear the people in the back whispering, "What's happening? What's He doing? Where's all that food coming from?"

The fact that the little boy's lunch contained barley loaves is seldom considered noteworthy. In Bible times, barley was held in low esteem. It was fodder for horses and camels, a symbol of poverty. It was worth less than one-third the value of wheat. How like Jesus to use this opportunity to illustrate the message of His kingdom in this incredible miracle.

The Creator of the universe was standing in the breadbasket of Palestine. He could have produced bread from the finest of wheat. He could even have called down manna from heaven! Instead, He chose to use a bread made from a grain looked down upon and scorned by the wealthier set. He blessed barley bread, processed by the hands of a simple peasant woman for her son's lunch. How like Jesus to not only reveal the kingdom by precept, but also by an illustration that

His audience would recall every time they sat to the table to break bread.

His message? "Blessed are the poor in spirit, for theirs is the kingdom of heaven." He wasn't saying that these people were spiritually depraved or deprived. On the contrary, He was complimenting the poor on their spirit of giving and sustaining one another. He welcomes their praise.

For thousands of years in the countries skirting the Mediterranean, barley has often been combined with black beans by peasant women to make a porridge. It is still prepared in this manner today. The recipe below is a modern-day adaptation of such a dish.

Barley Casserole

1 cup barley

3½ cups water

1 small onion, chopped

½ cup green pepper

½ cup carrots, chopped

1 cup celery

2 cups fresh or canned
tomatoes

salt and season to taste

2 cups shredded
cheddar cheese

Combine the barley, water, vegetables, and seasoning in a casserole dish. Bake the casserole covered at 350° for 60 minutes or until the barley is tender. When you remove it from the oven, sprinkle cheese on top. Then you can bake it 10 to 15 minutes longer to brown the topping.

Eggplant–Zucchini Parmigiana

"The peace of God, which transcends all understanding,
will guard your hearts and your minds in Christ Jesus"
(Philippians 4:7, NIV).

The summer before Richard left for college, he was dating Marianne, a pretty little strawberry blond in the neighborhood. As young as the lovely Marianne was, she knew Grandma's adage, "The way to a man's heart is through his stomach."

All summer long, Marianne plied him with freshly baked chocolate chip cookies. What young man could resist such delicacies? But, alas, summer ended. They said their goodbyes, kissed their last kiss, and he left for Atlantic Union College. That's where I entered the picture.

When Valentine's Day rolled around, the young women traditionally made heart-shaped cakes for their special guys. Since I abhor following the "herd," I chose to make him a double batch of cookies—chocolate chip cookies. For packaging, I made a heart-shaped box. To decorate, I whipped up a little clothing detergent with water and slathered it on the box like frosting. I added food coloring to the leftover "frosting" and wrote the traditional Valentine message on the top of the "cake."

After dinner that evening, I invited him to the dormitory kitchen, where I had ice cream and the "cake" waiting. When he tried to cut the cake, the cardboard resisted. Embarrassed, he tried again. I can only imagine what was going through his mind regarding my baking abilities and what he was going to say when my gift proved inedible.

After watching his several tries, I could no longer keep from laughing. Then I showed him the real treat, the cookies. We laugh to this day about the events that followed when he strode through the lobby of the men's dorm with this beautifully decorated cake. It didn't take more than one or two taking a swipe from the frosting for the news to spread regarding Richard's strange Valentine gift. Was it the cookies or my bizarre sense of humor that went to Richard's heart that day? Whichever, it proved to be a permanent condition.

"The way to a man's heart is through his stomach." For my grandma, that meant rich gravies, prime cuts of meat, and decadently delicious desserts. Today, I am wiser to serve meals containing less fat and less sugar to my darling Valentine.

Along the way, I've learned that if Richard's heart yens for good, old-fashioned eggplant parmigiana, I can satisfy it and satisfy the needs of his biological heart as well with this nonfry recipe.

Eggplant–Zucchini Parmigiana

1 medium eggplant,
sliced and halved

2 cups sliced zucchini

1 cup of low-fat cottage
cheese—drained

marinara sauce
(*see recipe page 37*)

½ cup shredded
mozzarella cheese

¼ cup grated Parmesan
cheese

In a large saucepan or Dutch oven, bring ½-inch of water to a boil. Add eggplant and zucchini slices. Cover and simmer for 4 minutes. Remove the slices from pan and drain onto paper towels; you may have to pat them dry.

In a casserole dish, line the eggplant and zucchini in columns, overlapping the slices and alternating the eggplant with the zucchini. Then spoon cottage cheese on top of the slices.

Pour marinara sauce over the cottage cheese surface. Finally, sprinkle it with mozzarella and parmesan cheeses. Bake it uncovered at 350° for 20 to 25 minutes.

Chinese Eggplant Steaks

On the first month anniversary of our marriage, I decided to prepare a romantic dinner for Richard and myself, beginning with soup and ending with dessert. Throw in soft music on the stereo, mood lighting, and a new negligee, and it would be an event to remember. Thirty plus years later, we remember it, all right!

In my attempt to create a chickenless chicken soup, I disregarded the recipe on the seasoning jar and instead, trusted my eye. Bad mistake. Several teaspoons of seasoning later, and I had a soup straight from the Salton Sea. I've never, before or since, tasted anything so salty.

A little salt goes a long way. The lesson stuck, not only in my stew pot, but in my witness, as well. Gentleness and restraint make both herbs and reproof more palatable. My husband, my children, and my friends, especially, appreciate this lesson.

This inventive veggie recipe calls for a light touch with the salt.

Chinese Eggplant Steaks

1 pound eggplant

salt

1 Tbsp. margarine or
butter

2 cloves garlic, chopped

2 Tbsp. soy sauce

1 Tbsp. rice-wine vinegar

2 tsp. sesame oil

½ tsp. sugar

¼ tsp. pepper (optional)

1 Tbsp. toasted pine nuts

1 finely chopped green
onion

One hour before you plan to serve, trim and discard the ends of an eggplant. Cut half-inch-thick slices, diagonally. Sprinkle both sides of each slice with salt, then place them in a colander and set them aside for 30 minutes.

In a small skillet, melt the margarine or butter over medium heat. Add garlic and sauté until golden. Then add soy sauce, vinegar, sesame oil, sugar, and pepper and cook for one minute. Remove it from the heat and spread the mixture into a large, shallow baking pan.

Rinse the eggplant slices and pat them dry. Place the slices in the marinade and turn each twice (to season). Set them aside for 20 minutes to 2 hours (whatever works for you).

When you're ready, drain the marinade from the pan and save it. Then broil the eggplant slices until they are lightly browned on both sides.

To serve this delightful dish, place the eggplant slices on a serving plate and top them with pine nuts and green onions. Reheat the marinade and pour it over the eggplant steaks. Then serve!

Rice Green Chili Cheese Bake

"I am come that they might have life,
and that they might have it more abundantly"
(John 10:10, KJV).

When Jesus spoke these words, He'd just healed Bartimaeus of his blindness, and the Pharisees were mad! This Nazarene was getting out of hand, uncontrollable. The fearful disciples turned to Jesus for words of encouragement. Instead, He warned them to beware, for thieves would come to break in, steal, and destroy all that He'd given them. If He'd stopped preaching then, with that warning, every disciple since—including you and me—would have cause to quake in our sandals. But He didn't. He saved the best till last. He said, "I am come that they might have life, and that they might have it more abundantly" (John 10:10).

When the Creator of the universe said He came to give us life, He took it beyond the "inhale-exhale" of living. That alone would be existence, not life. If He'd been writing instead of speaking, He would have typed the word life in all caps—LIFE! LIFE in Jesus is one that is exuberant, exciting, joy-filled.

However, He didn't just offer us life, even in the superlative. He added an incredible adverb—abundantly. Do you know what that word means? I thought I did, until I looked it up in my Bible dictionary. The word for "abundantly" in Greek is *hyperbole*. *Hyperbole*—don't you love it? For language aficionados like

113

myself, hyperbole means "gross exaggeration."

Another translator describes the term as "full and overflowing." Have you ever started filling a tub and been called to the telephone? And when you returned, the tub was beyond full. Water was cascading down the sides, across the bathroom floor, and onto the hallway carpet? Exceeding, beyond measure.

We all do it—hyperbolize, that is. When you tell your ten-year-old, "I've told you a million times to clean your room," you don't mean a literal 1,000,000. You are saying you've told him too many times. Hyperbole is a ten-foot tall hot fudge sundae. You describe your stack of monthly bills as a "mountain."

The disciples were frightened of what the Pharisees might do to them and to Christ. The Saviour wanted His friends to see beyond the immediate, to catch a glimpse of what life was supposed to be, what He came to give to those of us who loved Him.

He began by belittling the danger. "These things will happen; expect it. (Big deal!—my words, not His.) But I have come to give you life beyond measure, life in the hyperbole."

Wow! I like that kind of living. Read the book of Acts, and you will know that the Saviour kept His promise. The apostles were filled to overflowing with incredible joy. They encountered troubles, just as He promised, but they lived their lives in the hyperbole, praising God in the face of disaster and in the face of triumph. Paul and Silas made a jail house rock with their praises. Talk about life abundant!

A church potluck is an ideal place to visualize the word *abundance*. At our potlucks in Lindsay, California, the tables groan from the weight of hot sizzling casseroles, home-made breads, steaming vegetables, salads of every kind, and yummy desserts. And usually, because we live in the San Joaquin Valley, America's fruit basket, there is an abundance of colorful and exotic fruit; everything from kiwis to pomegranates to tangerines to die for! Add apples, peaches—the list goes on and on and on. Our choices are truly abundant.

If I didn't purposely wait until the end of the line so some of the more popular dishes would be gone, I'd fill my plate in the abundance as well. And I'm not writing this in the hyperbole!

However, if I see a bubbling Rice Green Chili Cheese Bake on the table, I will elbow my way up the line with the swiftest of them to get a dollop of this scrumptious casserole.

Rice Green Chili Cheese Bake

1 cup rice, uncooked

3 medium zucchini, sliced

2 cups sour cream

1 tsp. oregano

1 tsp. garlic salt

¼ cup green pepper, chopped

¼ cup onion, chopped

7 oz. can chopped green chilies

12 oz. jack cheese, grated

1 large tomato, sliced

salt to taste

2 Tbsp. parsley, chopped

Cook the rice as directed on the package. Cook the zucchini until it's al dente (crispy, tender). In the meantime, mix the sour cream, oregano, garlic salt, green pepper, and onion in a medium-size bowl and set it aside.

Put your rice into large greased casserole dish and cover it with chopped chilies. Sprinkle 1/2 the cheese on the chilies. Then spread zucchini slices over the cheese and tomato slices over the zucchini. Finish by sprinkling first with salt, then lightly with the remaining cheese. Bake the casserole at 350° for 40 to 50 minutes. Add parsley and serve!

Shepherd's Pizza Pie

"The Lord is my shepherd; I shall not want"
(Psalm 23:1, KJV).

We were sitting in a Mexican restaurant when Rhonda and Kelli told us. We'd placed our orders and were nibbling on chips and salsa when Rhonda withdrew an envelope from her purse and thrust it into her father's hands.

"Here," she said, "you'd better study this. You're going to England. We wanted to send you to Hawaii, but the overseas rates are better right now. This is yours and mom's twenty-fifth anniversary present." It was a brochure on touring London.

We were both stunned to silence. If you knew either Richard or me, you could better understand the significance of the moment. Neither of us is a person of few words.

When our reasons returned, Richard asked several intelligent questions, "But, how? Why? When?" Rhonda and her husband had just graduated from college, and Kelli was still attending. We'd been in a financial depression for two years, due to an unexpected job loss. Where had they gotten together the money for a gift so outrageous?

"We called all the relatives," Kelli informed us.

"You did what?" I was horrified.

"We called all the relatives and asked them to contribute." I was again speechless, and I must confess, I felt loved.

It was on this trip that I had the close-up opportunity to study sheep and shepherds—at least one shepherd.

We took a trip to the west country to visit Stonehenge, the place where these giant slabs of river rock stand perpendicular in a gentle, grassy hilltop, miles from their source. How they got there or why, no one knows for sure.

While we gazed at the circular monument, a shepherd passed by, beyond the enclosed area in which we stood. His sheep followed docilely behind—in a straight line. That's right, a straight line.

They weren't ambling close to his side or wandering about eating snippets of grass here and there, but one after another, they walked a narrow, well trod path, never deviating from that path. One sickly sheep stumbled and fell. His herd mates clambered over the top of the downed animal. Never breaking cadence to step around him or over him, they trampled him under their muddy hooves.

It was only when the shepherd noticed the fallen sheep that the procession halted long enough for him to rescue the injured animal. The other sheep grazed on whatever grass was close by. They weren't even inquisitive as to why the shepherd stopped or why he then carried the lamb on his shoulder.

Every time I hear the illustration of Jesus being our shepherd and "we like sheep have gone astray," I remember that day and the lesson I learned. And I ask myself, "Am I so intent on walking the straight and narrow that I trample those who fall by the way under my hooves?" And I praise God for a loving Saviour who, like the English shepherd, is always there to rescue me when I fall.

A shepherd's pie is a fun and healthy alternative to good old Italian/American pizza.

Shepherd's Pizza Pie
[MAKES 6 SERVINGS]

16 oz. package
hot roll mix

¼ cup instant
mashed potato flakes

8 oz. carton plain yogurt

½ cup water

1 egg

¼ tsp. salt

1 lb. ground gluten burger

olive oil

1 cup frozen peas and
carrots

2¼ cups shredded
mozzarella cheese

1 medium tomato,
chopped

½ diced onion

1½ tsp. Italian seasoning

milk

Combine the roll mix and potato flakes in a large mixing bowl, then set it aside. In a small saucepan, heat the yogurt and 1/2 cup of water until it's warm (120° to 130°). Then stir the yogurt mixture and the egg into the hot roll mix and potato-flake mixture.

Pour the whole thing out onto a lightly floured surface, knead it for five minutes, and finish by shaping it into a ball. Then cover it and let it rest for five minutes.

But you can't rest! First, add salt to the burger, then brown it in a skillet that has been lightly coated with olive oil. Stir in the peas and carrots, mozzarella cheese, tomato, onion, and Italian seasoning.

Now, roll out two-thirds of the dough onto a lightly floured surface. Shape it into a 13" circle and place it on a greased twelve-inch pizza pan. Top it off with the burger and the remaining cheese.

Next, roll out the remaining dough. Cut it into ½-inch strips to make a lattice top for the pie. Pinch both ends of the strips to bottom crust to seal them together. Finally, brush the dough with milk, then bake the pie at 400° for 30 to 45 minutes. Cover it with foil after 20 minutes to prevent a hard crust.

Spinach and Tofu Risotto

*"They received the message with great eagerness
and examined the Scriptures every day"*
(Acts 17:11, NIV).

Have you ever thought, "I hate studying the Bible. I want to like it. I know I'm supposed to like it, but it is s-o-o-o boring?" I have, many times. And something the pastor or my Sabbath School teacher would say would make me vow to get serious about my Bible study. I'd vow that this was the year I read my Bible through. And before President's Day, my carefully scheduled reading plan was shuffled through and lost in the clutter of my life.

My Bible study was kind of like eating plain tofu. I knew it was good for me, but taste? Eeugh! There was none. The slippery, squeaky substance set my teeth on edge. It was worse than gluten steaks without flavoring. However, once I tried a few tasty recipes blending tofu with other ingredients, I developed a taste for it. Now I enjoy it, and best yet, it's good for me!

It wasn't until I invited the Holy Spirit to show me God's will for my life, until He blended the ingredients of love, compassion, and promise as found in the Word that I learned how exciting Bible study truly can be. Now, I wonder how I lived so long without this heart-healing experience.

While this recipe for spinach and tofu risotto won't increase your enjoyment of studying your Bible, it's guaranteed to change your mind about tofu. The dish gets its protein from the tofu, rice, and cheese and is approximately 300 calories a serving.

Spinach and Tofu Risotto

8 oz. tofu, drained

½ cup chopped onion

1 clove minced garlic

2 Tbsp. cooking oil

14 oz. can tomatoes
(with juice)

1 tsp. dried oregano,
crushed

2 cups cooked brown rice

10 oz. package frozen
Italian chopped spinach,
thawed, cut up, and dried

½ cup shredded Swiss
cheese

½ tsp. salt

1 Tbsp. toasted sesame
seeds

Blend the tofu in your blender until it's smooth. In a large saucepan, cook the onion and garlic in hot oil until the onion is tender. Then add in the tomatoes (undrained) and the oregano. Bring it all to a boil and simmer it uncovered for three minutes.

Next, stir in the tofu, rice, spinach, 1/4 cup of the cheese, and salt. Place this mixture in a greased 1½ quart baking dish and bake it uncovered for 30 minutes in a 350° oven. Top if off with the remaining cheese and sesame seeds.

Turkey Day Loaf

*"Let us come before him with thanksgiving
and extol him with music and song"*
(Psalm 95:2, NIV).

In Acts 16, Paul and Silas put on an impromptu concert to a sell-out crowd. It rocked the rafters. As a result, the jailer and his entire family gave their hearts to Christ and were baptized. As a parent, I can relate to verse 34: "The jailer brought them (Paul and Silas) into his house and set a meal before them and the whole family was filled with joy, because they had come to believe in God" (NIV).

One of my greatest joys is gazing at the faces of those I love, gathered around our antique oak table laden with a holiday dinner. Holidays and the traditions that accompany them have always been a big deal around the Rizzo home.

One of the first family traditions we established in our home was holding hands as we pray. I treasure the moment when our hands and our hearts are linked together while Richard offers a blessing on our meal. The talk, the laughter, the food are important, but when we pause to pray—ah! How I treasure that moment.

Because we wanted our children to appreciate both my English heritage and Richard's Italian, we established the tradition of celebrating an English/American Thanksgiving and an Italian/American Christmas.

Every Thanksgiving meal must include mashed potatoes and gravy, my husband's favorite recipe for sweet potatoes, cranberry sauce, and, of course, turkey, at least my own version of the holiday bird. When the girls were younger, they would help me shape the roast like a bird. And just before putting our creation in the oven, they insisted we add two shortened dowels for legs. Today, the dowels are no longer necessary, but the "bird" is still a must.

Turkey Day Loaf
[**MAKES 7-10 SERVINGS**]

4 cups Special K cereal

1 cup onion, minced

1 can mushroom soup

3 eggs, beaten

½ cup celery, chopped

½ cup grated cheese

1½ cups cottage cheese

¼ cup oil

2 cups soy meat,
chicken style, minced

½ tsp. sweet basil

¼ tsp. garlic powder

1½ tsp. sage

⅓ tsp. salt (to taste)

2 six-inch wooden dowels

margarine for basting

Mix all the ingredients together (except for the wooden dowels!).

In a 9 x 11" baking dish, shape 2/3 of the mixture into an oval. Shape two smaller ovals on the lower half on each side of the large oval. Mold these two smaller one to resemble turkey legs. Insert the wooden dowels into the base of the smaller ovals, parallel with the large oval, leaving 1 inch of wood visible.

Baste the surfaces of your "bird" with margarine. Baste periodically during the baking process for a golden brown. Bake at 350° for 40 to 50 minutes. Happy Turkey Day!

Dirt Cake

"The Lord God formed man from the dust of the ground"
(Genesis 2:7, NIV).

I loved making mud pies and tea cakes as a child. My best friend, Patty Brown, and I would bake them in the sun. Then we'd gather our dolls and stuffed animals for a "tea party," al fresco. Our table would be a scrap board balanced on four rocks, and one of my mother's pillowcases would serve as a tablecloth. We'd have a center-piece of flowers: daisies, pansies, violets, dandelions; whatever was in season.

This memory would have hardly been unusual if one warm afternoon I hadn't dared poor Patty to eat a "tea cake." She did—one bite. Now, when I think dirt cake, I think of Patty Brown.

The first time I saw the recipe for dirt cake assembled, it was the dessert for a women's retreat in Redding, California. At each table setting was a "flower pot" with "gummy" worms crawling in and out of dirt cake. A silk sunflower sprouted out of the top.

Dirt cake can be a great summer table center piece by serving the cake in an unused clay pot, adding gummy worms and lady bugs, then topping it with a bevy of sunflowers. Scatter unused garden tools, packets of flower seeds, lots of red gingham and baskets across the tables, and you'll have a party hit!

Hmm, I think my friend Patty would have enjoyed this dirt cake much more than she did our regular garden variety.

20 oz. package Oreo cookies

1 cup chopped nuts (optional)

1 cup margarine

2 small packages instant vanilla pudding

1 cup powdered sugar

6 oz. nondairy whipped topping

8 oz. cream cheese

Gummy worms

silk flowers

Dirt Cake

In a blender or food processor, crush the cookies; then set them aside. Mix the nuts in with the cookies to your own taste. Now combine the pudding and the milk; then fold in the whipped topping and set this aside also.

Next, mix the cream cheese, butter, and powdered sugar. Then blend this into the pudding mixture. Beginning with the crushed cookies, layer the cookies and the pudding in a lined flower pot until it is nicely full. Then decorate the surface with gummy worms and silk flowers.

It sure beats a real mud pie!

Doughnut Rhyme

"Trust in the Lord forever, for the Lord . . . is the Rock eternal"
(Isaiah 26:4, NIV).

I love learning new things! Almost as much as I love learning old things! When I was researching for the *Chloe Mae Chronicles*, I found this old-time recipe. In 1851, Lucretia Allyn Gurney crossed the continent to homestead near Oswego, Oregon. With her, she brought the following recipe, not in a handy little cookbook, but in a rhyme memorized at her own mother's side. She passed the rhyme on to her children and grandchildren. A century and a half later, mothers might be reticent to prepare it too often for their children, but it still makes great fun reading.

The stories in the first part of the Bible were passed down, orally, from parent to child, until Moses' day when God commissioned him to write them down. They were a guide for living then, and they still are today. Over and over again, through the lives of His children, we can see that God can be trusted. Like Mama Gurney's doughnut rhyme, God's "recipe" for living has been tested and found to be reliable.

Doughnut Rhyme

"1 cup of sugar, 1 cup of milk,
   2 eggs beaten as fine as silk;
Salt and nutmeg, lemon will do,
   Baking powder teaspoons two;
Lightly stir the flour in,
   Roll on pie-board, not too thin.
[With a cutter, make the rings,]
   Drop with care the doughy things
Into the fat that briskly swells
   Evenly the spongy cells.
Watch with care the time for turning,
   Fry them brown just short of burning.
Roll in sugar, serve them cool.
   Price a quarter for this rule."

"A Taste of Oregon," Junior League of Eugene, Inc. 1982.

Honey-Granola Energy Bars

"How sweet are your promises to my taste,
sweeter than honey to my mouth!"
(Psalm 119:103, NIV).

Talk about love struck! I was one love-struck bride. I made a promise to love, honor, and respect my handsome Italiano. Today, I'm even more love struck than I was thirty-plus years ago. At twenty, I had no idea of how far the vows I took would take me.

My vow to love excluded any other "loves" that may come along. My vow to honor included listening with my heart, seeing with my heart, and trusting with my heart. My vow to respect restricted any sarcasm I might be tempted to direct toward him, any attempts to belittle him or our marriage—in private or in front of other people.

In a way, my marriage vows are similar to the vows I made to Jesus when I became His bride. The love, honor, and respect of this relationship is found in Exodus 20, the love commandments of God.

Every year, my marriage vows become sweeter and sweeter, like honey to my mouth. So, God's law, as I see its beauty working out in my life, grows sweeter and sweeter with every passing day.

Honey-Granola Energy Bars

½ cup sesame seeds

½ cup shelled sunflower seeds

¼ cup wheat germ

¾ cup honey

¾ cup peanut butter, chunky

3 cups oat flakes

½ cup nuts

⅓ cup dried prunes, chopped

⅓ cup dried apricots, chopped

½ cup raisins

Spread sesame seeds in microwavable dish. Cook uncovered in the microwave for 5 minutes. Stir seeds often while they cook; then set them aside.

Repeat the above procedure with the sunflower seeds, then the wheat germ.

Place the honey in a 2 qt. bowl and microwave it for 2½ minutes. Then stir in the peanut butter and cook it one minute longer.

Combine the sunflower seeds, wheat germ, honey mixture, oat flakes, nuts, prunes, apricots, and raisins. Mix them well.

Spread one-half of the sesame seeds on the bottom of a greased baking dish. Press the oat mixture into the dish. Sprinkle the remaining sesame seeds on top and press it all down firmly.

Chill the whole thing for an hour; then cut it into bars and wrap each one in plastic wrap.

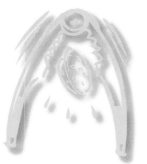

Peanut Butter Pizza

"What must I do to be saved?"
(Acts 16:30, NIV).

I grew up in an Irish/Catholic neighborhood in the '50s, where the aroma of cabbage cooking and sausage frying called the kids home in the evening. At school, I learned about Wiener schnitzel, German potato salad, and apple strudel.

As for Italian food, pasta in particular, I knew that elbow macaroni was the main ingredient in alphabet soup, in a salad, or in a casserole but never with a tomato sauce called marinara. And pizza? What's pizza? That and the foods of most other nationalities weren't in my vocabulary—let alone my experience.

The first time my father tasted Italian pizza was at an Italian wedding. My dad, a usually mild-mannered man, came home vowing it would be too soon if he ever ate another pizza pie again. 'Til the day he died, he never changed his mind, even after his younger daughter married an Italian.

As my husband and I moved around the country, we discovered a surprising number of variations from the tomato sauce and cheese pizza pie of the '50s. In California, it's pineapple on pizza; in Pennsylvania, sauerkraut; and in New Mexico, beans and chili peppers—different treats for different tastes.

Cynics claim that the Christian religion is like that, all offering the same basic ingredient—Jesus Christ—just with different toppings. One church offers baptism by water, while another offers baptism by the Holy Spirit. On the next block, a church has an active youth ministry, while another just built an impressive sanctuary.

These critics are right, if all they're talking about is religion. Religion is man's attempt to reach God, while true Christianity is God's efforts to reach man. And the critics are totally and sadly mistaken when confronted with true, life-changing Christianity.

True Christianity is a day-by-day relationship with Jesus Christ our Saviour and with the Holy Spirit living in us. This is far more than a variation on the original "pizza crust." Individuals find it to be ever-living, ever-changing, ever-growing. At the same time, a relationship with Jesus is the same today as it was when He strolled along the sandy beaches of Galilee or when He walked along the dusty roads with old Enoch. While my daddy may never have changed his mind about pizza, I'm so grateful he did about Christ Jesus. He dedicated his life to God when I was six years old. Four years later, I did the same.

Knowing my dad's penchant for peanut butter, I think he would have like this wild and wacky pizza.

1 pkg. yeast

1 cup warm water

2 tsp. honey

1 Tbsp. vegetable oil

1 tsp. salt

1 cup all-purpose flour

1 cup whole wheat flour

A handful of cornmeal

1 cup peanut butter

1 cup honey

¼ cup raisins

¼ cup sesame seeds

¼ cup shelled sunflower seeds

¼ cup coconut, shredded

¼ cup nuts, chopped

½ cup mozzarella cheese, shredded

Peanut Butter Pizza

[**MAKES 3-5 SERVINGS**]

In a medium-sized bowl, dissolve the yeast in water and stir; then set it aside for 10 minutes (until it's bubbly). Then stir in the honey, oil, and salt. Add flour and beat it until it's smooth.

Turn the dough out onto a lightly floured surface; add more flour if that seems necessary. Then knead it for 10 minutes. Roll out the dough to a 15-inch circle. Oil a 14-inch pizza pan and sprinkle it with cornmeal. Fit the dough onto the pizza pan. Press the edges of the dough to keep it flat; then set it aside for 15 minutes.

After waiting 15 minutes, bake the pizza dough at 450° for 15 minutes. Then remove it from the oven and lower the oven temperature to 350°. Combine the peanut butter and the honey; then spread it all over the pizza. Sprinkle the surface with raisins, sesame seeds, sunflower seeds, coconut, and nuts, and last of all, cheese.

Finally, bake your pizza at 350° for 10 minutes or until brown.

Scripture Cake

"A friend loves at all times"
(Proverbs 17:17, NIV).

When my friend Ann Miller heard about my plan to compile this recipe book, she sent me a copy of this recipe. Before you enjoy the humor in the recipe and its corresponding Bible texts, let me tell you about Ann.

Ann is one of those friends you keep for life. We first met in a little church in Troy, New York, when we were five and seven years old. (Guess who was older?) We attended the church school in the back of the sanctuary together.

When we both found ourselves in California, 3,000 miles from home and homesick, we drew together for strength. That was too many years ago to count. And she's still there for me. She never gives up on me. She's seen me through trouble. She's set me straight when I needed straightening. She's been a better friend to me than I have been to her, and she loves me anyway. I thank God for Ann. She's a treasure of a friend.

I hope you have fun with Ann's recipe for Scripture Cake. I had a hard time deciding if this recipe should be listed with the desserts or the "Just for Fun" section. You decide.

Scripture Cake

1 Kings 4:22
3½ cups sifted flour

1 Corinthians 5:6
2 tsp. baking powder

Leviticus 2:13
½ tsp. salt

1 Kings 10:10
¼ tsp. nutmeg

Revelation 18:13
¼ tsp. cinnamon

Song of Solomon 4:14
¼ tsp. allspice

Judges 5:25
1 cup butter or margarine

Jeremiah 6:20
2 cups calamus
(translation: cane or sugar)

Isaiah 10:14
6 eggs

Genesis 24:17
1 cup water

Exodus 3:8
3 Tbsp. honey

1 Samuel 30:12
2 cups raisins

Matthew 7:16
2 cups figs, chopped

Genesis 43:11
1 cup walnuts, chopped

Blend your flour, baking powder, salt and spices. Then, cream the butter and sugar in a large bowl until it's fluffy, then stir in the eggs. Sift 1/4 cup of the flour mixture into the large bowl and mix well. Then stir in 1/3 cup of water. Alternate adding the remaining flour and the water, stirring after each addition until the mixture is smooth. Then beat it by hand for 8 to 10 minutes.

Stir in the honey, raisins, figs and walnuts, then pour into a well-greased 10-inch tube pan. Bake it at 350° for 90 minutes. It's done when a toothpick inserted near the center comes out clean.

Earth Mother's Strawberry Shortcake

*"Train a child in the way he should go,
and when he is old he will not turn from it"
(Proverbs 22:6, NIV).*

"Earth Mother"—that's what my daughters called me. As a young mother of the seventies, I baked my own bread, washed my own gluten, and grew my own vegetables. Like many women of my generation, I assumed that my destiny in life was to be a "Proverbs 31" wife and mother.

However, the financial realities of the late seventies forced me to expand my thinking and cut back on my doing. With reluctance, I went back to college to complete my degree in English. On the way to graduation, I threw in an extra major—home economics. Why not? I certainly had the experience for it.

Once in my new job, I resolved never to let my busy teaching schedule interfere with my desire to "train up my daughters in the way they should go." My little darlings would become proficient at the same delightful skills of homemaking I enjoyed.

I tried, I really did. And at least once every spring, I declared that this would be the summer we, as a family, got "back to basics." My eyes would glisten when I described the quilt we would stitch and the garden we would grow. I could almost smell the aroma of homemade bread wafting from my kitchen stove once more.

Summer would arrive, and before I knew it, it was the middle of August, and we were back into another school year. My "back to basics" summer had to be stored away with the lawn mower and the garden rake.

Alas, in spite of my enthusiasm and instruction, Rhonda and Kelli shied away from the very domestic skills I believed to be indispensable to any woman. I was horrified to discover that the girls' ambitions were to become attaché-case bearing, cellular-phone wielding, career women of the eighties. They placed cookery, stitchery, and other domestic pursuits with bell-bottoms, plastic beads, and double-knit polyester suits.

"If at first you don't succeed . . ." I reasoned to myself. Abandoning my sublime arguments in the joy of domesticity for the practical, I reminded them that whether or not they married, whether or not they developed high-powered corporate portfolios, sooner or later they'd have to come home to an empty kitchen and a bathroom-in-distress.

Their naive replies ran from "I'll have a maid" to "I'll marry a man who likes to cook."

"Yeah, right!" I nodded my head and rolled my eyes.

"Face it, Mom. We'll never become happy little homemakers like your generation."

Somewhere during their late teens, I gave up. While I still required them to do their share of the household chores, I stopped harassing and accepted the inevitable—I'd failed.

Then one Friday night in June a few years later, when we were in the middle of a three-way conference call between Rhonda's place in Portland, Kelli's apartment in Walla Walla, and our home in Santa Cruz, Rhonda mentioned that she and her husband had enjoyed fresh strawberries with homemade shortcake for supper.

My jaw fell to the floor. Richard tapped his ear, then the phone, sure that one of them was malfunctioning. Before I could say a word, Kelli broke in, her voice ringing with excitement, "Hey, Mark and I did too. I picked up a pint of berries on my way home from classes this afternoon." Her voice rose with enthusiasm. "What recipe did you use for your shortcake? I used Betty Crocker's."

"I got mine out of my *Better Homes and Gardens* Cookbook." Rhonda continued. "I thought about buying a package of those mushy little cupcakes, but I like the ones made from scratch much better."

Kelli was in complete agreement. "I know what you mean. It takes no time at all to whip up the batter and pop them into the oven. And you know they have to be much better for you."

Richard and I just listened in stunned silence as our two undomesticated daughters chatted on about the benefits of baking from scratch.

Betty Crocker lives! I thought. The words, "by precept and example" popped into my mind. More by example than precept, I decided.

I'm afraid Rhonda's and Kelli's perspectives had changed with maturity and not with my admonishments. I was relieved to discover that neither had espoused the superwoman syndrome of the eighties, but had found a way, as women of the nineties, to combine their career goals with the values they'd inherited from the "earth mother" generation.

As I thought about Solomon's advice, I am certain he was thinking more of growing strong mature Christians than making strawberry shortcake. Perhaps though, the process is the same. Trust in God is learned through example. Obedience to God is learned by imitation. Faith in God is learned at the knee of the faithful. And service to God is learned by seeing and doing.

While, sometimes, as parents, it seems our lessons dissolve in a sink full of dirty dishes, or our wise counsel is tossed out with yesterday's trash, a wise Father reminds us that our efforts are not wasted. The proverb talks about the beginning and the end but makes no mention of the days, months, and years in between.

Children sometimes wander down strange pathways. Parents' knees may develop calluses from long hours of praying, and their tongues may be scarred from biting back uninvited counsel. Yet, it is the happy parent who lives to enjoy the fruits of her efforts, which just may include homemade strawberry shortcake!

Earth Mother's Strawberry Shortcake

[**MAKES 6-8 SERVINGS**]

2 cups flour

3 tsp. baking powder

1 tsp. salt

2 Tbsp. sugar

6 Tbsp. shortening

⅔ cup milk

strawberries
(sweeten to taste)

Heat your oven to 450° (hot). Sift the flour, then mix the dry ingredients well in a bowl. Cut in the shortening until the dough looks like "meal." Next, stir in the milk until your dough is puffy and easy to roll out. Finally, cut it into 2½- to 3-inch rounds and bake for 10 to 12 minutes.

Break the shortcake rounds apart while they are still hot. Place the bottom half on a dessert dish and spoon on the sweetened strawberries. Top it off with the other half; then add more berries. Serve with plain or whipped cream. Quick, easy, delicious!

Grandma's Oatmeal Cookies

*"My grace is sufficient for you,
for my power is made perfect in weakness"*
(2 Corinthians 12:9, NIV).

Elvira Rizzo is one of the most beautiful women I've ever known. Gracious and loving, strong and full of enthusiasm, she can't do enough for others. She'd give away her last dollar to help someone in need, and her coat as well.

She came to visit our home a few years ago. With her living in Florida and we in California, her visits are few and precious. As I watched her indomitable spirit, I wondered, *How did she become this way?*

Then I remembered her childhood. Her mother died when Elvira was eighteen months old. Because her widowed father couldn't handle a toddler, he took her to live with her grandmother and grandfather. Later, after he remarried, she was raised in a convent school because her stepmother resented having the child in the house. She looked too much like her husband's first wife, Elvira's mother.

At the convent, she learned that to be liked she must make herself useful. She learned to cook, to sew, and to do embroidery—all the things she'd need to become a successful wife and mother. She learned everything, except how to love.

When she discovered and accepted the presence of Jesus in her life, the Creator filled that need first with His love, then with the love of a husband and three children. Over the years, He took Elvira's weakness and turned it into her strength. She loves in adversity. She loves in censure. When rebuffed, she loves. When mocked, she loves. When belittled, she loves. She knows her Jesus and is confident in His love for her. That puts everything else into perspective.

She showed her love to Richard and me recently by making, then sending, us a care package of his favorite cookies—not just any oatmeal cookies, but Grandma's oatmeal cookies. Eighty-eight years old and she's still showing her love in the best way she knows how—doing for others.

Grandma's Oatmeal Cookies

½ cup walnuts
(finely chopped)

½ cup raisins

2 cups flour

1 cup oatmeal
(quick cooking)

4 tsp. cinnamon

½ tsp. baking soda

¼ tsp. salt

¾ cup Crisco shortening

1 cup sugar

2 eggs

¼ cup milk

In a small bowl, mix the walnuts and raisins; then set them aside. In a second bowl, measure out the flour, oatmeal, cinnamon, soda, and salt; then set that aside.

Place the Crisco shortening in a large mixing bowl; then add the sugar a little at a time, mixing as you go until it's creamy. Then add one egg at a time, mixing well between eggs until the mixture is fine and even creamier.

Add the flour mixture, a little at a time, mixing as you go, until the batter seems too dry. Then add the milk until you get just the right consistency. Then you're ready to stir in the walnut/raisin mixture.

Drop teaspoon-size clumps of this cookie dough onto a greased cookie sheet and bake in your preheated oven at 350° for 12 to 15 minutes. Then remove and enjoy! (I didn't want you to forget that part!)

Gingerbread Nativity

"Glory to God in the highest,
and on earth peace, good will toward men"
(Luke 2:14, KJV).

Each year, on December 1, the nativity set appears; first, in front of the fireplace; then later, under the tree. For evening worship when the girls were young, Kelli, Rhonda, and I would lie on the floor on our tummies at eye level with the plastic characters and talk about the story of Jesus' birth. They would choose a different character each night, and I would weave a story around the painted figurine, what brought him to the stable, and how he felt about the newborn baby. Even the donkey, sheep, and cow had their turns. When we ran out of characters, we repeated the girls' favorites. We saved Jesus' story for last.

On Christmas Eve, after Richard read from Luke 2, I repeated the stories of the month, with Rhonda and Kelli supplying the details I'd forgotten.

Though the girls are absent, the plastic nativity characters reappear every December 1. And though Mary's robe is no longer peach and Joseph's brown cloak is chipped, the precious memories of those evenings are fuzzy with love and affection.

When I began assembling this cookbook, I considered including the recipe and pattern for a gingerbread church the girls and I created one Christmas. But, the memory of reliving the Christmas story through the sparkling eyes of my daughters sparked a better idea. I would change the gingerbread village to a gingerbread nativity set.

Imagine telling the story of Jesus' birth as you and your children cut out forms representing each of the participants. What an opportunity to share the beautiful story of God's love for us.

If you choose not to eat your masterpiece, the birds will love your generosity once Christmas passes.

Gingerbread Nativity

⅓ cup soft shortening

1 cup brown sugar (packed)

1½ cups dark molasses

⅔ cup cold water

7 cups flour

2 tsp. baking soda

1 tsp. each:
salt, allspice, ginger,
cloves, and cinnamon

. . . .

Decorator icing:

1 cup sifted confectioners'
sugar

¼ tsp. salt

½ tsp. vanilla (or lemon,
almond, or peppermint)

1 to 2 tsp. water
(whatever it takes to thin
the icing enough to push
it through the pastry tube)

tint (if desired)

Mix the shortening, brown sugar, and molasses thoroughly. Then stir in the water and sift in the flour. In another bowl, blend all the other dry ingredients together—then stir them into the shortening mixture. Chill the results in the refrigerator.

While it chills, cut out patterns for each of your gingerbread figures (*see pages 150-152*). Then preheat your oven to 350°. Roll out the dough ¼-inch thick and trace around the pattern pieces—this makes it easy to cut around the pieces with a knife. When each piece is cut, transfer it to a lightly greased cookie sheet with a pancake turner.

Bake the gingerbread for about 15 minutes or until the light touch of your finger leaves no imprint. Allow it to cool slightly; then carefully remove it from the baking sheet. With the decorator icing in a pastry tube, add the desired details to your creations.

Decorator icing:
Blend the ingredients and spread or squeeze through tube onto cookies. Let it dry before any little hands touch it!

For "gluing" the stable pieces together, add egg white to a small amount of the icing. Brace the pieces together two at a time until the "glue" hardens.

------- Suggested decoration

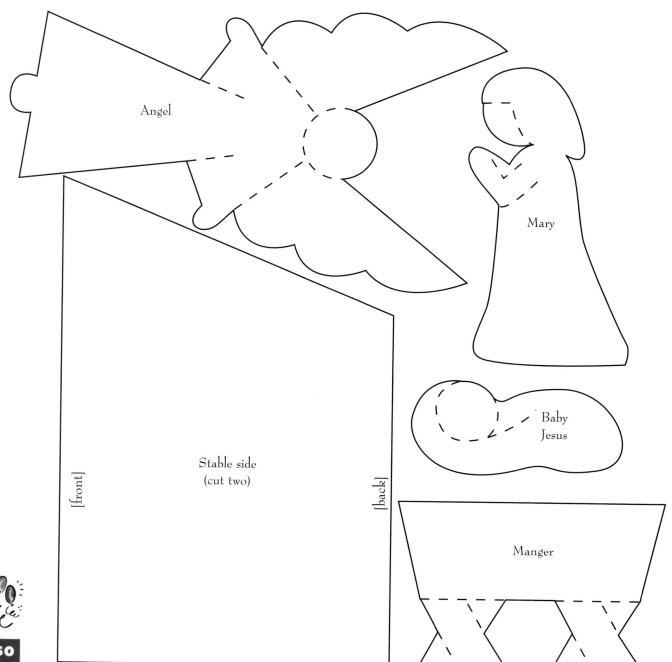

Angel

Mary

Stable side
(cut two)

[front]

[back]

Baby
Jesus

Manger

150

Shepherd

Lamb

King
(cut three)

Joseph

Donkey

Stable back wall and roof
(cut one for each)

Example of assembled nativity scene

Rainy Day Fun

"Take time out to play"
(Rizzo 1:10).

Message to young parents: Take it from a 50 plus-year-old mama—if I could change the past, if I could return to the days when my children were tiny, I would:

1. Complain less.
2. Ban "people pull-apart" from our diet.
3. Play more. (And not necessarily in that order!)

Complain less. How I wish I'd known the beauty in the principle of praise, both of God and of my loved ones! What a difference it could have made. But, in God's time, I have discovered praise, and it has changed my life.

Banning the game of "people pull-apart" (criticizing and gossiping) would have projected to my children the importance of respecting others, no matter who they were, and would have curbed the cynicism so prominent in their generation. Such a ban could have made their pathways much smoother and would have brought more joy to our table.

As to the play, I did that right. My only wish, as I look back on our short time together, is that I'd taken more time to get down to their level and simply enjoy them.

Kelli always had a creative bent, an imaginative spirit. She could "see" life in anything. When we'd go for walks, she'd come home with rocks, sticks, and other exotic treasures. Once a month, when it became time to do a thorough house cleaning of her closet, I'd toss out her collection, and when I wasn't looking, she'd sneak out back and rescue it from the trash can.

She could play with a bag of clothespins for hours. A tin of buttons could keep her busy all afternoon.

Rhonda was more project-oriented. She needed goals to keep her focused. One of her father's greatest treasures is a sampler she embroidered with his ham radio call letters.

But both girls especially loved it when I took time out from my work to play with them. This happened often on rainy days. Looking back, I'm also glad videos hadn't yet been invented.

Here are a couple of ideas that both the girls and I enjoyed on rainy days in the big woods.

Silly Putty

white glue
(Elmer's won't bounce or
pick up pictures)

Sta-Flo™ liquid starch

food coloring

Mix 2 parts glue to 1 part liquid starch. Let it dry until it feels workable. Add a few drops of food coloring for color. You have to store this in an air-tight container.

Bubble Stuff

⅓ cup dish soap

1½ cup water

2 tsp. sugar

drop of food coloring

plastic straw

Combine these ingredients and pour it all into a container. Use the straw to blow the bubbles!

Finger Paint

3 Tbsp. sugar

½ cup cornstarch

2 cups cold water

food coloring

liquid detergent

4 or 5 jars

Mix the sugar and cornstarch; then add to the water. Cook it over medium heat, stirring constantly until it's blended. Then divide the mixture into the small jars. Add a drop of different colored food coloring to each jar. Add a drop of dish detergent for easy cleanup!

Simple Finger Paint

shaving cream

dry poster paint

white paper

Spray shaving cream on a piece of white paper. Sprinkle dry poster paint on the cream and let the child go for it!

Dough Art

[**FOR OLDER CHILDREN**]

2 cups flour

1 cup salt

1 cup water

model paints

Blend together the flour and salt; then add the water a little at a time. Knead this dough 7 to 10 minutes until it's firm. Next, pat the dough to the desired thickness. Mold or cut out designs (cookie cutters can be used). If you decide to make hanging decorations, be sure to poke a hole through them for the string before baking.

Bake the results at 325° for 35 to 60 minutes, depending on thickness. If air bubbles develop during baking, stick a needle into them. When the designs are cooled, paint the details on the hardened forms.

Have fun with your kids—they won't be little for long!

Notes

Notes

 Notes